Shrubs for the Garden

Shrubs for the Garden

John Cushnie

Photography by Marianne Majerus

KYLE CATHIE LIMITED

To Laura, Simon, Richard and Ash
with love

First published in Great Britain in 2004 by
Kyle Cathie Limited
122 Arlington Road
London NW1 7HP
general.enquiries@kyle-cathie.com
www.kylecathie.com

ISBN 1 85626 502 1

© 2004 John Cushnie
Photography © 2004 Marianne Majerus
See also other copyright acknowledgements on page 224

Project editor   Caroline Taggart
Design   Caroline Hillier
Copy editor   Selina Mumford
Editorial assistant   Vicki Murrell
Production   Sha Huxtable and Alice Holloway

A Cataloguing in Publication record for this title is available from the British Library

Printed and bound in China by C & C Offset Printing Co Ltd

half-title Ruscus hypoglossum
opposite title page Genista aetensis growing with Rosa 'Ballerina' *and echinops*
title page Hibiscus syriacus 'Lady Stanley'
this spread, background Hedera helix f. *poetarum*
opposite Skimmia japonica berries in winter

Contents

Introduction

opposite GARRYA ELIPTICA decorated in winter with male catkins.   *above* HYDRANGEA MACROPHYLLA 'ALTONA'

S hrub is a lovely word, sliding between the teeth with a soft landing to conjure up the image of a sumptuously bushy plant. Shrubs help to mould a garden, adding colour, shape, texture and fragrance, and complementing trees, bulbs, annuals and perennials. They are enormously resilient, well capable of tolerating changeable climatic conditions, inadequate soil, vandalism and neglect. That is not to say they won't respond to some tender, loving care, and if they are fed and watered they will be happy to put on their best display.

As a basic working definition, 'a plant with multiple woody stems rising from ground level' describes a shrub pretty well. There is no maximum or minimum height – 15cm (6in) high heathers are shrubs, while some varieties of escallonia will grow to 4m (13ft) in height. Shrubs can be deciduous or evergreen, but either way they usually have conspicuous flowers. The fruit may be delicious or toxic. In addition to their role in the border, shrubs are in demand as formal or informal hedges to shelter, screen and protect. Low-growing evergreens such as *Cotoneaster* x *suecicus* 'Skogholm' and *Hebe pinguifolia* 'Pagei' make ideal ground-cover plants to prevent weeds growing.

In other words, there is a shrub for every garden, every season and every need. The trick is to find the right one for your purposes.

Choosing a shrub

Ask yourself what you have to offer a potential new shrub. Of course you are hoping to give it a good home, but what do you mean by that? Is the area where the shrub is going to live in sun or shade, sheltered or windy? What type of soil will it have to tolerate – wet, dry or in-between? Alkaline or acid? As with all plant groups, there are some that can put up with almost anything and others that are more fussy, but even if all you have to offer is cold, wet, acid soil in shade under a tree, you can grow *Ledum groenlandicum*, with its dwarf, rhododendron-like habit and pure white flowers in late spring. The majority of shrubs are middle of the road, happy in most soils and climatic conditions. They show their displeasure by wilting or dying when they are suffering in the extremes of acid or alkaline soil, boggy or bone-dry ground or unsuitably high or low temperatures. To give you an example, gardening in Northern Ireland makes it difficult to give lavender what it likes best, which is a free-draining, impoverished soil with lots of sun and a dry atmosphere. Regular pruning prolongs its life but eventually it becomes woody and after between six and seven years I tend to put it out of its misery.

The most important piece of information to glean before buying is the shrub's ultimate height and spread. Will there be space for the plant to develop? Will it be crowded and its shape spoilt by nearby plants? The suggested spacing may seem to be generous when planting, but two buddleja planted 3m (10ft) apart in spring will be touching by the following autumn.

◆ Other questions to ask yourself concern maintenance. How much of it do you want to do, and how skilled are you? Some shrubs, such as forsythia and philadelphus, require annual pruning to guarantee flowers. Others, including rhododendron, magnolia and hamamelis, may never need to be touched. If you've never pruned a shrub before, there are instructions on pages 16–17, and in the directory details are given under each plant.

◆ Think about evergreen versus deciduous. The latter loses its foliage in winter, but its autumn leaf colour may be spectacular.

◆ Season of flower is important, especially if the garden is mainly used and enjoyed in summer and early autumn.

A summer show of *Lavandula stoechas* subsp.
pedunculata 'James Compton' in a border with alliums.

◆ Fragrance is often a bonus, especially from shrubs that dish it out rather than forcing you to bury your nose in the flower. *Sarcococca confusa* produces tiny white flowers in winter that dispense fragrance over a wide area.

◆ The stems of shrubs can be striking. The bright red bark of the deciduous dogwood, *Cornus alba*, or the contorted hazel, *Corylus avellana* 'Contorta', with its twisted branches and winter catkins, are wonderful, but they must be pruned every spring.

◆ If you have young children plants with toxic fruit or berries must be banned from the garden. Unfortunately such shrubs include *Daphne mezereum* with its super-fragrant, deep pink, late winter flowers, followed by bright red fruit. Be patient and plant this treasure when the children are older.

◆ Check before purchase that the plant is container grown rather than containerized, complete with a ball of roots that can tolerate transplanting.

◆ Once you have selected and bought the right shrub, plant it in its permanent position in the garden as soon as soil and weather conditions permit (*see pp.12–13*).

Well-mixed evergreen and deciduous shrubs: *Cornus alba* 'Sibirica' and *Euonymus fortunei* 'Silver Queen'.

Shrub Care

CLEMATIS ARMANDII

A modicum of basic knowledge, a little bit of effort and a pinch of common sense go a long way with a shrub. They may make the difference between a plant that struggles or sulks throughout its life and dies before its time, and one that is resilient enough to withstand pests and diseases while giving pleasure for many years.

The way a shrub is planted is one of the factors that will determine its future. Ensure that its roots can function properly in suitable soil. As they spread out and down they should be able to absorb nutrients and water. If your soil is poor – or if you resolve to grow a particular shrub whether you have the ideal conditions for it or not – you will have to work all the harder to keep it healthy and happy. Giving adequate space for it to grow to maturity should result in a well-shaped plant, without the dead and brown foliage caused by congestion.

Routine watering during dry periods, regular attention to pest and disease control, an annual or twice-yearly application of fertiliser and pruning to shape the shrub, ensure that you get rid of unhealthy growth and encourage flowering wood and are all part of shrub care.

If you care for a shrub properly, it will more than repay you. Trust me.

Planting a shrub

Planting is like making compost – neither should be rushed if you want a good end result. Digging a hole, setting in the plant and covering the roots is the basic principle, but for the long-term health of the shrub the operation needs to be refined.

When to plant

A shrub growing in a container such as a black polythene bag or a rigid plastic or clay pot may be planted at any time providing the soil is in good condition (*see pp*.14–15). Avoid cold, wet soil that sticks to the spade and your boots. Some deciduous shrubs may be on sale in winter as plants dug from the field without any soil on their roots. These need to be planted as soon as possible to prevent the roots drying out. If the site hasn't been prepared or if the ground is sodden or frosty, they should, as a temporary measure, be heeled into moist sand or soil with their roots covered. Firm the soil to eliminate air pockets around the roots.

1 Make the planting hole at least twice the size of the pot or roots. Dispose of any subsoil.

2 Loosen the soil in the base and sides of the planting hole with a digging fork to allow roots to penetrate and water to drain. Spread a layer of old farmyard manure in the base and add bonemeal fertilizer.

3 If the roots are tangled or congested gently tease them out of the rootball.

4 Place the rootball in the hole, keeping it at the same depth as in the pot. Fill with topsoil, firming in layers to prevent air pockets forming.

5 A final firming of the soil with the foot. Slope the soil towards the plant to collect water.

6 Water the shrub to settle the soil around the roots.

7 Mulch with compost or bark to conserve moisture and reduce weed germination.

Tips for successful planting

◆ Whenever possible, form a planting hole at least twice the size of the root area or container. Separate the subsoil from the darker topsoil. Fork up the base and sides of the hole to loosen the soil and allow water to drain away. Doing this will enable the roots to penetrate the soil in search of nutrients and to anchor the plant.

◆ Spread a layer of well-rotted farmyard manure in the base of the planting hole and mix a handful of bonemeal through the pile of excavated topsoil.

◆ Water the compost before lifting the plant from its pot.

◆ When you are ready to remove the plant from its container, take care not to disturb the rootball. Check to see if the roots are congested. If they form a tight ball, gently tease them out without causing damage. With bare-root shrubs trim off any broken roots with a sharp knife. Arrange the roots to spread in every direction to help hold the plant in place.

◆ Set the plant in the hole at the same depth as it was in the pot. Spread the roots out and backfill with topsoil. Firm the soil as you fill the hole to exclude air pockets, which would allow the roots to dry out and die.

◆ Fill the hole to the top and firm with your foot to prevent the shrub rocking in the wind. Make a dish shape in the surface of the soil so that the sides slope down towards the plant and help retain moisture. Water the plant well after firming to settle the soil. Discard the subsoil.

◆ Water regularly until the roots are established and can take up water. If the plant is large, establishment may take up to six months. A surface mulch of shredded bark will help to conserve moisture and stop weeds germinating.

◆ When planting more than one shrub together, remember to check their ultimate spread and leave sufficient space between plants for them to grow without crowding each other.

Fertilizer

Nutrients serve different purposes and they are available in various forms. The two most popular fertilizers are formulations sold either as a liquid to be diluted or in a granular form to be incorporated into the soil or scattered around the plants. The three main nutrients and their symbols are nitrogen (N), phosphate (P) and potash (K), frequently referred to as NPK.

Nitrogen encourages speedy growth, making it ideal for leafy crops such as cabbages and leafy hedges. Apply it reasonably early in the season, because if you leave it too late the resultant soft growth may be killed by frost and cold winds.

Phosphate encourages a good root system.

Potash is essential for the development of flowers and fruit, and if applied mid-season it will harden up new growth and make it better able to withstand frost. It also helps plants to resist diseases.

Trace elements such as magnesium (Mg) and iron (Fe) are usually present in the soil. Some shrubs, including roses, are greedy for the minor nutrients and rose fertilizers, which contain trace elements, and should be given to these plants.

Established shrubs planted in the ground will be content with two feeds per year, one in spring as growth commences and again in autumn before the plant slows down for winter. For shrubs growing in ornamental containers as permanent plantings, more regular watering and feeding will be necessary. In these cases, the roots can't go in search of nutrients and soon the compost in the container will be drained of food.

Weeds & weeding

The golden rule is to plant into clean ground that is free from perennial weeds. It sounds simple but most nasty weeds are dormant during winter and only very close attention to the soil, as it is being cultivated, will highlight their roots. By spring those that have been missed will carpet the ground, competing and choking the life out of young shrubs later in the growing season. If you don't mind using chemicals one of the quickest and most effective methods of weed control is to apply glyphosate weed killer. It is a systemic chemical entering the weed through the leaf, travelling down to the roots and killing the plant. For

Compact-growing *Acer dissectum atropurpureum* in autumn. Planting a single shrub in a small bed like this can brighten up an otherwise dull patch of paving.

tough weeds such as horse tail and convolvulus more than one application will be required to eliminate the weed. Bear in mind that if this chemical is sprayed onto the foliage of a shrub it will kill or maim it, but it won't harm hard, woody stems bare of foliage.

Organic growers won't want to use chemicals but can achieve excellent results by placing old carpet or landscape fabric covered with gravel, slate or bark mulch on the soil, covering all the ground between plants. Daylight is necessary for the manufacture of chlorophyll and by excluding light for long periods all plants, including weeds, will be weakened. Regular hoeing to keep on top of annual weeds works well when the soil is dry. Take care with the hoe blade in the area of the shrub's roots as some, such as philadelphus and lilac, have roots close to the soil surface.

To lessen the chances of the weeds spreading it is important to remove them before they set seed. When digging out perennial weeds such as dock and convolvulus it is important that as much root as possible is found and burnt. Please don't be tempted to put seeding weeds or the roots on the compost heap.

Planting specimen shrubs

Where an instant garden is demanded or large shrubs are required for immediate screening, then buying from a nursery specializing in semi-mature, container-grown plants is the answer. The cost will be high but, providing the shrubs are well grown and in large containers, they will provide the desired impact. Give some thought to the ultimate height and spread of the plant. It will continue to grow after planting and while you planned for it to be a 3m (10ft) high shrub you may not be happy if it eventually reaches double that height.

If the rootball is solid with tangled roots you will have to tease them apart prior to planting. Water the planting hole before setting in the plant. A large plant may need to be tied to a stake to prevent it from blowing over. After planting firm the soil with your foot and water well to settle the soil around the roots. A 5cm (2in) deep bark mulch will go some way to preventing water loss through evaporation.

Pruning

When it comes to pruning, shrubs fall into three categories: those that need an annual pruning; shrubs that must be cut back to keep them within their allotted space; and the group that will perform for some years without pruning but will be all the better for regular secateur work.

Pruning serves several purposes. It promotes growth, but more importantly it builds up a framework of flowering stems. By removing old, less productive branches the plant's energy will be diverted to the new shoots. To keep the shrub looking attractive and well balanced, crossing branches should be cut out. And finally, diseased wood must be pruned out to prevent the risk of the infection spreading.

When to prune

The right time to prune depends on when the shrub flowers and whether it does so best on the current season's growth or that of the previous year. Forsythia flowers in early spring on growth made during last summer. For maximum show prune this shrub immediately after it has finished flowering to keep it in shape and to allow new growth to be produced in summer. Philadelphus, better known as mock orange, flowers in early summer. Treat it in the same way as the forsythia, but as it has less time to make new shoots, prune it the moment its flowers and their fragrance fade. *Hydrangea paniculata* 'Grandiflora' flowers at the height of summer on young shoots produced since spring of that year. It is best to prune the previous year's growth in spring.

Why would you want to prune a magnolia, rhododendron, pieris or camellia? It is only necessary to cut them back if they are taking up too much space. Left to their own devices they will cover themselves with blossom. Cotoneaster, mahonia and hebe can be ignored for years and will still put on a good annual

1 Cut out diseased and dead branches well below the infected area.

display. Eventually, however, they will become straggly and produce fewer flowers. There is sometimes a case for rejuvenating old shrubs. Some plants such as rhododendrons, escallonia and olearia will produce new growths from old branches that have been cut back to stumps. These tend to look bare and unsightly for a few years and there is the argument that a new plant will make a better specimen more quickly.

2 *left* Remove crossing and rubbing branches.

3 *right* Some old shrubs can be rejuvenated by cutting out the main branches close to ground level.

Pests & diseases

Everything that lives must die, and the lifetime of a plant depends upon the suitability of the soil and climatic conditions, but freedom from pests and diseases will undoubtedly extend its life. The best advice I can offer is not to worry unduly about either pests or diseases. Sometimes they can be a real pest, if you know what I mean, and occasionally a disease will cause plants to die. Usually, however, they are a nuisance, looking worse than the actual damage they cause. A few chewed leaves or brown spots aren't worth treating. There are, however, pests such as slugs, and diseases, including canker, that go from bad to worse and these should be treated before the damage becomes serious.

Protect plants from larger animals such as rabbits, hares and deer which chew the bark of shrubs; where it encircles the main stem the plant will eventually die.

COMMON PESTS

Aphids are commonly called greenfly but may be brown, yellow, grey or even pink in colour. These pests are 2–3mm (1/8in) in size and cast their skin as they grow. They are sap suckers, preferring young, new shoots especially towards the tip. Aphids are responsible for transmitting virus disease, which can cause distortion and mottling of the foliage. Roses and honeysuckle are prone to attack. A sticky honeydew is excreted onto the lower leaves forming a black and mouldy layer called sooty mould.

Control Use a systemic insecticide at two-to three-week intervals; to treat organically apply insecticidal soap.

Caterpillars of various moths and sawfly hide in rolled up leaves or form a silky-tented web. They chew their way through masses of leaves making a visual mess of the shrub without causing permanent damage.

Control Garden birds offer good control as they peck off the caterpillars and eat them. Picking off and burning the affected leaves will reduce the population.

Leaf miners are small, white grubs that tunnel through the leaf between the upper and lower surfaces leaving a silvery, wavy trail. The leaf may blister and if the infestation is heavy it can look unsightly, but there will be no lasting damage. An attack on holly foliage can look quite dramatic.

Control It is seldom worth spraying with a systemic insecticide. Removing and burning the occasional infected leaf is sufficient control.

APHIDS

CATERPILLARS

above LEAF MINERS   *below* RED SPIDER MITE

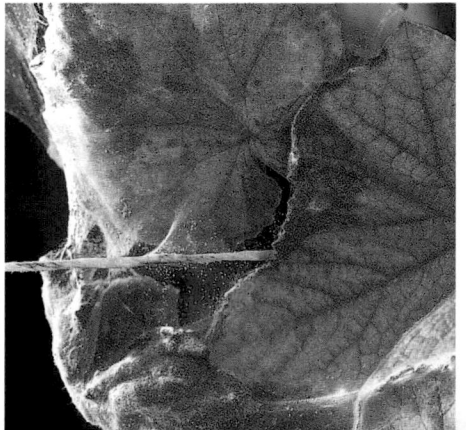

SLUG DAMAGE

ADULT VINE WEEVIL

above BLACKSPOT   *below* CANKER

Red spider mites are minute arachnids visible as an orange-cream dust on the underside of leaves. Don't let their size fool you, as an attack will cause the leaves to discolour and fall. Bush roses and the blue spruce are particularly susceptible.

Control Red spider mites dislike a moist atmosphere so regular damping over the plants in summer will reduce attacks.

Slugs and snails feed on young stems and leaves but are only of nuisance value on mature shrubs. They are most active at night and mark their presence by leaving silvery slime trails. During the day they can be found under stones and among the branches of dwarf box hedging. Another favourite hiding place is on ivy-covered walls.

Control Trapping them using beer, milk or grapefruit skins is a successful method of control. They can be deterred by surrounding plants with coarse grit or copper strips. Container-grown plants are safe if the rim of the pot is smeared with vaseline or a similar greasy substance, preferably one specially made for this purpose.

Vine weevil is a serious garden pest. The creamy-white larvae will eat the roots of a young shrub, curbing its growth or killing the plant. The adult beetle appears at night eating leaves and leaving its trademark of serated and notched leaf edges. Heavy attacks will leave mature rhododendron foliage in a mess.

Control Biological control using nematodes is a successful way to keep this pest within bounds. Chemical treatment may be justified for young plants.

COMMON DISEASES

Blackspot is a fungus disease mainly attacking roses. Rapidly spreading small, black, round spots appear on the leaves, which turn yellow and fall prematurely. The spores of the fungus overwinter on the stems and on decaying foliage lying on the ground.

Control A hard pruning in spring and a deep surface mulch helps to reduce recurrence. Some modern rose varieties are less susceptible to blackspot.

Canker is a killer disease. The fungus or bacteria enters the plant tissue through a wound. The bark of an affected shrub is discoloured and may be sunken or weeping. As the canker encircles the branch the area above the infection dies.

Control Remove diseased stems, cutting well below the area showing infection. Make a clean cut without ragged edges. Applying a fungicidal wound paint to larger cuts will reduce the risk of infection.

Coral spot can be recognized by raised orange-red pustules on dead, woody branches followed by dieback, which spreads down the stem eventually killing the plant. This disease is caused by a fungus that lives on dead material including pea sticks and enters the plant via a pruning cut or physical damage. The spores are produced all year and are spread by water or rain splash.

Control Cut out the affected stem cleanly, well below the infected area and burn the prunings. Elaeagnus, Japanese maples, sycamore and magnolias are particularly vulnerable to infection.

Fireblight is a bacterial disease and its common name adequately describes how a diseased plant looks, as if it has been scorched by a flame. The flowers wilt and turn black and the leaves become brown and then black with cankerous areas on the stem. During periods of wet weather these diseased patches ooze a bacterial slime. Individual branches die while others remain healthy for a season.

Control Remove infected branches, cutting at least 60cm (24in) below the damage. Make sure you clean the secateurs before cutting into healthy wood. Eventually the whole plant dies and should be removed and burnt. Members of the Rosaceae family such as pyracantha and cotoneaster are particuarly susceptible. There is no cure and in Northern Ireland it is still a notifiable disease.

Honey fungus kills woody plants and is one of the most serious of all tree and shrub problems. Affected shrubs can die over a few weeks or struggle for up to two years. A sign that the plant is under attack is if it fails to leaf up in spring or if it collapses during summer with the foliage dying on it. There are several indications of the possible presence of honey fungus. Between the bark and the woody tissue of infected plants there will be a layer of creamy-white, mushroom-scented mycelium. Black fungal strands of rhizomorph also form in the surrounding soil, giving rise to the common name of bootlace fungus. These travel through the soil until they come in contact with a suitable woody host, which they live off and kill. Groups of honey-coloured toadstools may appear at the base of the plant in late summer or autumn.

Control Honey fungus is difficult to control. Immediate removal by the roots of infected plants will slow it down. Healthy plants can be protected by forming a solid barrier in the soil surrounding them using 1000 gauge polythene sheet in a trench 45–50cm (18–20in) deep. Make sure the polythene is at least 5cm (2in) above the surface of the

CORAL SPOT

above FIREBLIGHT *below* HONEY FUNGUS

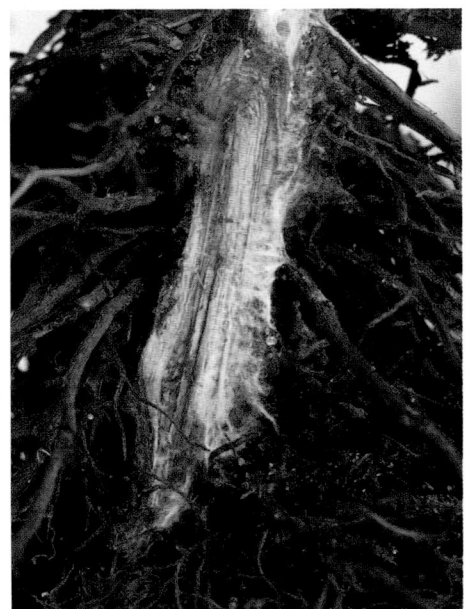

PHYTOPHTHORA

VIRUS

soil to prevent the fungus 'jumping' the barrier. Some shrubs appear to have a degree of resistance to this disease. Bamboo, chaenomeles, choisya, elaeagnus, pieris and sarcococca are worth trying.

Phytophthora is a root-killing fungus that travels through the soil and is carried by water. Symptoms include yellowing of foliage followed by parts of the shrub dying. Eventually the whole plant is killed. A red-brown discolouration is usually visible under the bark at soil level. Conifers, heathers and hardy hybrid rhododendrons are particularly susceptible.

Control Dig out dead plants with as much root as possible and burn. A preventative measure is to ensure that the ground is well drained, making drains if necessary.

Virus comes in many different forms. Some will kill a young shrub while others disfigure by distortion and mottling of the leaves and stunting the plant. They can be spread by sap-sucking insects such as aphids. Only propagate from healthy shrubs.

Control Dig out and burn infected plants.

Using chemicals safely

◆ Keep chemicals locked away when not in use and well out of reach of children.

◆ Store all insecticides, fungicides, weed killers and fertilizers in a well-ventilated, dark, cool, dry room.

◆ Never transfer chemicals into unlabelled containers.

◆ Read the label and dilute, applying to the shrubs as recommended.

◆ Only apply chemical sprays during calm weather, preferably in the early morning or in the evening when bees are in their hive.

◆ Wear protective clothing including goggles, gloves and a waterproof outer layer when working with chemicals.

◆ If chemicals are splashed onto your skin wash the area well with cold water.

◆ Don't store chemicals beyond their sell by date.

◆ Never get rid of old containers of chemicals in the wastebin with domestic rubbish. Telephone your local authority to seek advice about their disposal.

Propagation

SOFTWOOD CUTTINGS
1 Take a heel cutting using a sharp knife.

Reproducing plants by sowing seed is great fun and you get a sense of satisfaction producing your own plants from start to finish. If the seeds are sown in the ground the total cost is the price of a packet of seeds. However, I get a 'feel good' buzz when I manage to propagate a plant from a cutting. I feel confident a seed will become a seedling and then a plant if given the right conditions, which is its purpose in life, but with a cutting it is different. Left to do its own thing a section of plant without roots will wither and die, and to succeed in getting it to root and grow into a replica of the parent plant is worthy of self praise. It is reassuring to know that the pieces of plant you root will be identical to the original plant.

The golden rule is to never take a cutting from a garden you are visiting without getting the owner's permission. There are shrubs that are difficult to root, such as Japanese maples and daphne, but others including hebe, philadelphus, weigela and euonymus root like weeds with guaranteed success. A heated propagator with soil warming cables and a misting unit is definitely worth using for stubborn plants, but for most, inserting the cutting in compost, watering and covering with clear polythene to retain moisture is all that is needed. There are many ways to propagate shrubs including softwood, semi-ripe and hardwood cuttings. Layering, stooling, budding and grafting can be tried with the minimum of equipment and a little knowledge.

2 Remove the lower leaves and the growing tip.

3 Trim the heel, then dip the base of the cutting in hormone rooting powder.

Seed

When harvesting seed from the garden remember that the resulting plants may not be the same as the parent plant; for instance plants from the seed of a red rose will be mixed in colour. There may be a winner among the thousands of seedlings but you will have to be patient and wait for two years until they flower – good luck.

Seed may be sown in pots of compost in the greenhouse or on a windowsill in the house where there is plenty of heat, moisture and

4 Insert in compost around the inside rim of a pot.

5 Water and cover with a clear polythene bag.

6 A well-rooted cutting.

light. Sowing outdoors in the garden soil is generally slower with a risk of cold, wet conditions and snails and other pests waiting to taste the seedlings as they emerge. Sow the seed thinly in rows and lightly cover with soil, always labelling the rows. After germination thin the young plants or transplant them to allow them space to grow.

Softwood cuttings

These are taken from the current year's growth in late spring or early summer. Pull a side shoot off with a heel of the older stem. Next trim the heel, remove the lower leaves, and then nip out the growing tip and any flower buds. Alternatively, take a 5–10cm (2–4in) piece of stem without a heel and cut cleanly immediately just below a leaf joint. Remove the lower two leaves to discourage rotting and nip out the growing tip as before.

Fill a clay or plastic pot with a compost of equal parts peat (or a peat substitute) and coarse sand. In a 15cm (6in) diameter pot there will be room for between 10 and 12 cuttings. Dip the base of the cuttings in hormone rooting powder or gel and insert them 3–5cm (1–2in) deep and 2.5cm (1in) apart around the inside of the pot. Label the cuttings and water the compost thoroughly. Cover the pot with a clear polythene bag and seal it to retain moisture, but make sure the foliage isn't touching the polythene as the moisture may cause it to rot. Some cuttings will root within a few weeks and others may take much longer. Once the plants start to grow making new leaves they are ready to be transplanted. Move them into individual pots, taking care not to damage the brittle roots as they are being separated. Water and grow on under cover for a season. Harden the plants to the outside conditions before planting in permanent positions in the garden.

Semi-ripe cuttings are propagated in much the same way as for softwood cuttings. The difference is that the cutting material is selected at the height of summer when it has had time to firm up.

Hardwood cuttings

This is by far the simplest method of propagating shrubs because there is no need for compost, rooting powder or protection from the elements. Take the cuttings in late autumn or winter, selecting stems of this year's growth. Cut the stems into 30cm (12in) lengths discarding the soft growth at the tips. Next dig a 15cm (6in) trench in a sheltered part of the garden and line its base with a 2.5cm (1in) layer of grit to improve drainage. Insert the cuttings 15cm (6in) deep, 10cm (4in) apart, the right way up, in the trench and backfill. Firm the soil with your foot and water to settle the soil around the cuttings. Be sure to keep the area weed free. They will root during the following year and produce side shoots. Twelve months later the well-rooted young shrubs will be ready to dig up and plant out into the garden in their permanent positions or potted up to grow on in a container.

HARDWOOD CUTTINGS

1 Prepare the cutting by removing the leaves and nipping off the soft growth at the tip. Trim to 30cm (12in).

2 Dig a 15cm (6in) deep trench and add a layer of grit to its base.

3 *right* Insert the cuttings 10cm (4in) apart in the trench. Finished job.

LAYERING

1 Select a low branch that will easily bend to touch the ground.

Layering

There are many plants that can prove difficult to root by cuttings, but the good news is that they can often be rooted by layering; these include camellia, chaenomeles, cotinus, hamamelis, kalmia and rhododendron.

In a way you could call it cheating to propagate by layering, as the shrub does all the work. The principle is simple – select a branch that can be bent to ground level. To prepare the ground dig over the soil, adding compost or peat. Where the branch comes into contact with the soil make a long shallow cut part-way through the stem using a sharp knife and wedge the wound open with a matchstick. Dust the area with hormone rooting powder. Use two U-shaped wires, one on either side of the wounded area, to hold the branch in place on the ground. Form a mound of well-worked soil or compost over the wound. Water generously and cover with a large stone or concrete block to secure the plant and help retain moisture in the soil. After about a year carefully ease the branch out of the ground. It should be well rooted and ready for separating from the parent plant. Please think twice before making the cut, as you would not be the first gardener to cut the branch on the wrong side of the roots. You now have a large shrub ready for planting out.

2 Partially cut the branch to form an open wound.

3 Peg the branch securely in the soil.

4 Cover with compost and a stone.

Stooling and dropping

Stooling and dropping are both forms of layering. To propagate
by stooling heap up the soil around shrubs with upright branches
such as philadelphus, ribes and deutzia. Cut back the stems in
winter to 2.5–5cm (1–2in) above soil level. Earth up the new
shoots as they appear, as you would a potato plant. Eventually
mound the soil to a depth of 20–25cm (8–10in), but never cover
the shoots completely. In winter remove the soil and each stem
will have its own root system. Cut them off and plant out or pot
up, leaving the stumps and repeat the process.

Dropping is the opposite of stooling and is ideal for heather.
Dig up a mature clump. Deepen the same hole and add well-
rotted farmyard manure. Sink the heather plant into the hole
keeping the tops of the shoots above soil level. Cover the plant
with a mixture of peat, grit and fine soil, working it through the
stems of the heather with your fingers. Water well to settle the
soil. In about six months lift the clump carefully out of the
ground. All the newly rooted stems can be cut off and potted up
making good-sized plants within a season.

Budding and grafting

For these methods of propagating more skill is required. The aim
with grafting is to get a piece of one plant to join itself onto
another plant of the same genus. Budding is where an individual
bud of a particular rose variety is attached to a common rose
rootstock grown from seed. This form of propagation allows
breeders to quickly multiply their stock of a particular variety.
The rootstock will give vigour to the variety.

top Stooling *Philadelphus* 'Sybille' results in
a mass of well rooted cuttings.
below *Rosa* 'Irish Eyes' budded onto a rose
rootstock.

Designing with Shrubs

EUPHORBIA CHARACIAS SUBSP. WULFENII 'JOHN TOMLINSON'

Of all the plants we grow in our garden shrubs are the most versatile. Many other plants, while fantastic in their season, let us down for long periods each year. Bulbs are indispensable, making an excellent display when in flower, but their glory is short lived and the beauty of annuals can be measured in months. Borders of herbaceous perennials are stunning in summer but can look miserable in winter. Trees are magic and every garden should have at least one but their numbers are naturally restricted in small spaces. Shrubs give us much more. Even the variety of foliage, which comes in two times forty different shades of green, can offer an exciting canvas on which to superimpose seasonal colour. The diversity shrubs provide in shape, texture and size makes them so useful in the garden. While some grow as big as trees others slither over the ground in ever widening mats. In between there are shapes and sizes to fit every garden.

Planning the border

When designing a shrub bed or border it is helpful to draw the area on squared paper, using a scale that will allow the whole area to fit onto the sheet. When you have decided on the shrubs you want to plant, mark them on the plan. Make sure that they are spaced correctly, taking into account their ultimate height and spread. At maturity they should be touching but not overcrowding their neighbours. Packing plants into a confined area will result in all of them being spoilt. Evergreens will lose their foliage where they are congested and those that are most vigorous will smother slower-growing plants. When properly spaced there will be gaps for a few seasons with bare earth showing until the plants reach their ultimate size, but these areas can be filled, on a temporary basis, with cheap and cheerful annuals and perennials. As the shrubs spread, the fillers can be removed. At worst they will be smothered with no ill effects on the permanent planting. Don't be tempted to buy more plants than your plan dictates as in the long term there will not be enough room to house all of them.

Positioning plants

Taller 'dot' shrubs spaced at intervals throughout the border will provide height to contrast with the low, edging shrubs along the sides. With borders that back onto walls or hedges and can only be viewed from one side it is important that the plants are not in competition and blocking one another. Such plantings need to be carefully planned with tall-growing plants like leycesteria, escallonia and forsythia planted to the rear of the bed. *Viburnum rhytidophyllum* and *Berberis* x *stenophylla* are two tall shrubs that flower at the same time and make a stunning combination. The contrast of the enormous, evergreen viburnum leaf and the dark green, needle-like, evergreen leaf of the berberis highlights their differences. Medium-height shrubs can be planted in the middle of the border with lower-growing shrubs such as hebe, dwarf rhododendron and euonymus to the fore. It is possible to add some height to the front of the bed providing the shrub doesn't swamp its smaller neighbours. Fastigiate conifers such as *Juniperus scopulorum* 'Skyrocket' are great as punctuation marks.

From the ridiculously small-leafed *Berberis* x *stenophylla* to the sublimely large-leafed *Viburnum rhytidophyllum*, there is a shrub to fit every mood and every taste.

Mixing & matching shrubs

This style of planting can be great fun and usually succeeds. Allowing climbers such as clematis to scramble through shrubs such as shrub roses or pyracantha can be charming. There is the possibility of combining clematis with plants that flower at the same time such as roses, *Choisya ternata* or philadelphus. Alternatively, if a clematis flowers when its host supporter is out of season its display will be extended. A mature sea buckthorn, *Hippophae rhamnoides*, gives clematis plenty of room to manoeuvre around. I have the pleasure of watching *Clematis alpina* with its blue and white flowers mixing with *Amelanchier lamarckii*. Often it comes into bloom as the deciduous leaves of snowy mespilus, the name given to all amelanchiers, are turning from bronze to dark green, but at other times the alpine clematis flowers in time with its clusters of white flowers. In my garden *Fuchsia* 'Riccartonii' and hazel are totally untroubled by *Clematis* 'Royal Velours' as it scrambles over and through their framework making a glorious show for the camera. It is essential the companions are compatible and that, in time, a vigorous climber won't overpower and smother its support. Mixing deciduous and evergreen shrubs is another effective way to add variety to a bed or border.

right The strong reds of *Fuchsia* 'Riccartonii' and *Clematis* 'Royal Velours' are a perfect backdrop for this exotic dahlia, 'Arabian Night'.

below *Clematis* 'Royal Velours' climbing through *Hippophae rhamnoides* (sea buckthorn). The main reason for growing sea buckthorn is its display of bright orange autumn berries, but its delicate grey-green foliage is a great foil for this rich, velvety clematis.

Year-round interest

Any garden worth its salt will be able to provide interest and colour all year round. One of the easiest ways to achieve this is to use 'all round' shrubs. *Mahonia* x *media* 'Charity' has interesting foliage for twelve months of the year, winter flowers and berries and not a minute goes by when its popularity slips. Its evergreen, 45cm (18in) long, pinnate, glossy, dark green, sharply toothed leaflets emerge at the tip of the shoot as a cluster of soft bronze, cup-shaped leaves spreading to their full length before turning green. The highly fragrant racemes of winter flowers are primrose-yellow and are followed by blue-black berries. *Cornus alba* 'Aurea', while deciduous, manages to keep itself busy. Its soft, butter-yellow leaves make a wonderful contrast to dark foliage during summer. After leaf fall the younger, bare stems with their bright red bark seem to glow in pale winter sunlight. *Pittosporum tenuifolium* 'Tom Thumb' is another great all-round plant with its evergreen, crinkly, bright green leaves that become deep purple as they mature.

A little colour goes a long way in winter and, for me, that is important. I love to dander round the garden in the worst of the weather, and with protective clothing against rain, snow or a heavy frost nothing can stop me from going outside to see a hamamelis or chimonanthus with its flowers outlined in frost. The flowers of mahonia, daphne and sarcococca are unaffected by extreme weather and continue to manufacture wonderful fragrance in all conditions and it is definitely worth venturing out to see and smell these garden delights.

There is nothing so impressive as a border of mixed shrubs that can be viewed from both sides. With knowledge and imagination it is possible to ensure there is leaf and flower colour all year round. A selection of shrubs should provide flowers throughout the four seasons with different leaf colours and shapes. Autumn leaf colour, winter coloured bark and fruit will help to keep the garden interesting from one moment and season to the next.

Good use of hard and soft landscape materials: pebble mosaic contrasting with a clipped *Pittosporum tennifolium* 'Tom Thumb', *Alchemilla mollis* and *Lavandula* 'Munstead'.

Colour in the garden

When it comes to colour in the garden I am convinced we can get away with any combination that pleases us. In the home you have to be so careful with paint, wallpaper and curtains while in the garden, as far as I am concerned, pink, yellow, white, orange, purple and blue fit together well. It may be the backdrop of the many shades of green foliage that neutralizes colours but whatever the reason, mixed colour planting seems to work.

I once spent a night in a bedroom where the wall paper was an unfortunate blend of purple and orange. The purple was a washy pink-violet and the orange wasn't ripe, with a hint of green. Sleeping with the light off was a pleasure. In the garden there seldom are colour clashes and after this episode I deliberately planted a *Clematis tangutica* with its bell-shaped, yellow-orange, late summer flowers and let it scramble through a group of *Hydrangea macrophylla*. These mopheads flower in a range of colours from dusky pink through mauve to red purple. In late summer and autumn the clematis and hydrangea give a spectacular combined display and, for me, it is a perfect example of colour harmony in the garden. The silky seed heads of the clematis are an added bonus as the hydrangea flowers fade to silvery-pink. Pinks and reds don't always mix well indoors but in the garden these colours, in the form of climbing roses, look at home draped over a pergola or an archway. To make the summer display even more charming plant a few summer-flowering clematis and a couple of honeysuckles.

Grey-green or silver foliage has a calming effect on bright colours and to tame gaudy red or shocking pink flowers to acceptable shades plant them close to or among *Chamaecyparis lawsoniana* 'Gnome' or *C. lawsoniana* 'Minima' and silvery-grey leafed senecio. Bright sunlight tends to tamper with colour adding a hint of yellow to all flower colour. In the evening, as the red in the sun's rays intensifies, bright colours lose their strength becoming mellow and warm.

Keep the backdrop in mind when planning a colour scheme, particularly if it is solid such as a brick or painted wall. Certainly, on a bright sunny day, mauve or orange flowers fronting a red brick wall will glare at you. Bright-flowering shrubs look much better against foliage. A dark green yew hedge or the purple of *Berberis thunbergii* f. *atropurpurea* will highlight and magnify any yellow-flowering shrub. *Cytisus* x *praecox* and *Genista lydia* will make a better show against a plain-leafed background rather than green and yellow variegated foliage. Be careful not to overuse coloured foliage. A clump

Cytisus battandieri looks good with the foliage of *Corylus maxima* 'Purpurea'.

of purple, red or yellow is fine but when such shrubs are dotted around they break up the overall look and feel of the garden causing you to view it as a series of mini pictures rather than as a whole.

It is difficult to state with any certainty exactly when a shrub will flower, as so much depends on climatic and soil conditions. The quantity and type of nutrients available in the soil will influence flowering time, as will the age of the plant. These factors can upset the best-laid plans for a colour scheme with, for example, a blue-flowering shrub blooming ten days ahead of its yellow-flowering neighbour. To guarantee colour at all times, where space allows, plant a group of the same shrub. The resulting bold splash will be more dramatic than single dots of colour. Most landscapers, garden designers and books on garden design recommend group planting in odd numbers of say three, five or seven. I can see no advantage to this and an even number of the same shrub planted in a group will be every bit as effective, providing they are not in a straight line.

Shrubs for the border

The garden border is where you may let your imagination run riot. A good mixture of shrubs will provide colour, shape and texture. Every plant must be able to stand up for itself and not be ignored or passed without comment because of showier neighbours. It must mix well without overpowering or smothering nearby plants. Suckers of plants such as viburnums, roses and *Hypericum calycinum* tend to become weeds, sneaking among other shrubs and becoming established before you can eliminate them. I would tend to plant them as specimens, or at least somewhere where you can keep an eye on them and remove the suckers as soon as they appear.

Plant tall-growing deciduous varieties with arching branches such as the mock orange (*Philadelphus*) towards the centre of the border. In winter their bare stems will allow light to reach underplanted evergreen foliage. Upright or dwarf shrubs belong at the front of the border where they will be too polite to trespass over the path or lawn. One of my favourite plants for a border is *Cytisus* 'Killiney Red', a broom with masses of red flowers. It is a great plant for late spring and early summer. Prune it immediately after it has finish flowering to encourage new growths for next year's bloom. This prevents the pendulous growths tumbling over the other plants. For a well-behaved shrub with spectacular perfume in late winter and early spring, choose the deciduous *Daphne mezereum* 'Bowles' Variety' syn. *D. m.* 'Bowles' White'. The pure white clusters of early flowers exude their heady fragrance irrespective of the weather. The variety 'Alba' has creamy-white flowers.

Hydrangea paniculata is a big, bold, deciduous shrub with mid-green leaves and large, conical panicles of creamy-white flowers in late summer and early autumn. There are few other late summer-flowering shrubs that will make the same impact in a border. Another good hydrangea is *H. aspera* subsp. *sargentiana*, also referred to as *H. sargentiana*. It is deciduous with velvety, dark green leaves and thick, bristly stems. In late summer and autumn the heads of flowers are as large as dinner plates with purple or blue flowers surrounded by an outer ring of white flowers.

The Persian lilac, *Syringa* x *persica*, forms a bushy shrub with dark green, deciduous leaves and panicles of highly fragrant, purple flowers in late spring. The whole family of viburnums is worth growing, but for something a little different plant *Viburnum davidii* towards the front of the border. Its large, deeply veined, glossy, dark evergreen leaves make a wonderful backdrop for the small, white, tubular flowers in spring. It produces

Used properly, shrubs and perennials are happy bedfellows, as in this combination of *Rosa* 'The Fairy', foxgloves, *Buddleja davidii* 'Harlequin' and *Macleaya cordata* (plume poppies).

magnificent metallic-blue fruit. *Lespedeza thunbergii*, bush clover, is a subshrub dying back to ground level in cold areas. The blue-green, deciduous leaves are held on arching shoots and its pink-purple flowers appear in late autumn and trail down in terminal racemes.

Island beds

A well-designed, planted and maintained bed in a sea of grass is a joy to behold. As it matures it gradually changes, becoming more defined with an air of permanency. Shape is important. Island beds are usually designed in flowing curves, which enable you to hide small plants that only become visible as you walk round the bed. Crescent, ink blot, pear, kidney and tear drop shaped beds work but it is essential that the curves are gradual to allow the lawn mower to be effortlessly taken round the perimeter. Where the planted island is to be observed from an upstairs window, mark out the plot and see how it looks from above as a shape that appears ideal at ground level may be totally wrong when seen from a bird's-eye view. Rather than making the bed in the centre of the lawn, offset it in the one third that is most distant from the dwelling. Stepping stones can be set into the grass curving to the island and continued through the planting to the far side, inviting you to explore further.

When selecting and positioning the plants in your bed always remember that it can be viewed from all angles. Large island beds will benefit from height in the form of a fastigiate conifer or a small tree such as the golden Irish yew, *Taxus baccata* 'Fastigiata Aureomarginata', or *Prunus* 'Amanogawa', the flowering cherry tree, which has an

Hebe 'Red Edge' forms a compact evergreen mound, ideally suited for the front of a shrub bed.

A group of *Genista hispanica* will soon form a continuous spread of colour.

upright habit. 'Weeping' plants, such as the eye-catching *Fagus sylvatica* 'Purpurea Pendula' with its glossy, deep purple foliage, also make a statement.

Choose plants that as a collection will provide colour and shape for most of the year. The little evergreen holly, *Ilex crenata* 'Golden Gem', is a real star. It loves full sun where its golden-yellow leaves seem to glitter. It is reluctant to flower but when it does, black berries are produced. Its low-growing habit makes it ideal for either side of stepping stones or tucked into a sunny curve hidden from view by larger plants. *Hebe* 'Red Edge' is another low-growing evergreen and it forms a dumpy mound of grey-green leaves margined with red. The spikes of lavender-blue flowers appear in summer. *Leptospermum humifusum* has a habit of changing its name; it is also labelled *L. rupestre* and *L. prostratum*. In its native Tasmania it is known as the tea tree. Evergreen and prostrate, its small leaves are a glossy deep green. The star-shaped, white flowers are carried in profusion from late spring until mid-summer.

Every bed needs a duvet cover and what better than the most trouble-free heather I know. Mat-forming *Erica carnea* 'Springwood White' flowers in late winter and early

spring. If a group of them are planted 45cm (18in) apart they will quickly form a white carpet with bright evergreen foliage. To add some variety plant a few E. c. 'Springwood Pink', which is identical in habit with bright pink flowers that age to a deep pink.

Rhododendron 'Vuyk's Rosyred' is an evergreen hybrid azalea. In mid-spring it will clothe itself with a mass of deep rose-pink, funnel-shaped flowers with a darker pink blotch on the inside. Another great rhododendron from Japan is R. yakushimanum, which is sometimes called R. yak. The glossy, dark, evergreen leaves are reddish-brown on the underside. In mid-spring the pink buds open to form trusses of up to ten, funnel-shaped, rose-pink flowers that fade to pale pink or white.

above Erica carnea 'Springwood White' forms a snow-white carpet.

right Rhododendron 'Vuyk's Rosyred' is guaranteed to flower every spring.

Shrubs for edging paths

This is a lovely route to go down providing the plants are set back from the edge so as not to over grow onto the path, causing restricted movement. On a hot summer's day it is very pleasant to brush against an edging of aromatic foliage and smell its fragrance, but that same path on a cold, wet day is less inviting. Where the path is a main passageway for wheelbarrows and bulky loads be sure to leave plenty of space for access. Shrubs that are naturally compact and those that tolerate regular clipping are ideal for edging. A well-manicured box hedge is an example of where tight, bushy plants work. More lax, tumbling shrubs will soften the edges, blurring the defined line to either side or flowing over a raised kerb or brick edging onto the path. Avoid bushy evergreens, which tend to open up as they get older. *Hebe rakaiensis* is one such culprit – it always grows to be a larger mound than you imagined and then falls apart, opening its bare centre to the heavens. Evergreen shrubs will identify the path better than plants that

below *Euonymus fortunei* 'Emerald 'n' Gold' provides year-round colour.
right The foliage of *Prostanthera cuneata* gives off the aroma of mint.
The flowers are pretty, too.

are devoid of foliage in winter. When selecting plants for this purpose bear in mind that slow-growing varieties will require less maintenance than those that grow quickly with a spreading habit.

Here is a selection of shrubs ideal for edging a path. *Euonymus fortunei* 'Emerald 'n' Gold' and its mate *E. f.* 'Emerald Gaiety' are compact, bushy, variegated evergreens. The foliage of 'Emerald 'n' Gold' is bright green, margined with yellow. 'Emerald Gaiety' will form a larger plant with white-edged leaves. With both varieties the variegation turns pinkish in winter. *Gaultheria mucronata* 'Bell's Seedling' has small, sharply pointed, glossy, dark evergreen leaves held on stems that are red when young. This bushy plant is laden with large, dark red berries in autumn and winter. Being hermaphrodite there isn't a sex problem! *Prostanthera cuneata* hails from Australia. It is commonly known as the alpine mint bush and for good reason. Close your eyes, rub the small, cupped, glossy, mid-evergreen leaves and smell its minty fragrance. White flowers with purple and yellow marking appear in summer. One of the best behaved edging plants is *Cotoneaster congestus*. It is mound-forming with pale, evergreen leaves and bright red fruit. Rosemary is one of the more useful herbs so if it is planted close to a path it is easy to pick for the Sunday lamb. *Rosmarinus officinalis* makes an upright plant with aromatic, leathery, dark evergreen leaves, which are white on the underside. Blue-purple to white flowers appear in late spring and early summer and again in autumn. There are numerous varieties including *R. o.* 'Miss Jessopp's Upright' and *R. o.* 'Prostratus', which is dwarf but not very hardy. *Erica arborea* 'Estrella Gold' is an evergreen tree heath with small, lime-green leaves tipped bright yellow. The white flowers appear in spring.

If you edge a path with rosemary (*Rosmarinus officinalis*), you'll release the beautiful fresh scent of its aromatic leaves every time you brush past. Being Mediterranean in origin, rosemary does best in mild areas, but can cope with cooler climates if planted in a pot and positioned in a sheltered spot.

Shrubs for foliage

When used in small doses the leaf colour of shrubs can outshine the brightest flowers, deciduous shrubs will perform continuously for up to seven months, and evergreens all year round. For this reason foliage shrubs, particularly variegated, have to be incorporated into the planting plan with care. Too much foliage and it may become boring, remaining unchanged for month after month.

Yellow

We use the word yellow to describe a broad band of colours from pale lemon to deep orange-gold with butter-yellow in the middle. Deciduous shrubs with yellow foliage play an essential part in the garden palette. They can brighten the dullest corner and are useful for drawing the eye to a particular area. Most yellow-leafed plants prefer a position in light shade, as the glare of full sun tends to lighten the colour and at worst scorch the foliage, turning it to a crispy brown. Ideally plant in an open woodland situation where the rays of the morning and evening sun will spotlight the foliage and the shrub will light up the surrounding area. In a mixed border, these plants are particularly successful when combined with the rich purple foliage of *Cotinus coggygria* 'Royal Purple' or blue-flowering shrubs such as the deciduous or evergreen ceanothus.

Here is a selection of my favourite yellow-leafed shrubs. *Acer shirasawanum* 'Aureum' forms a bushy shrub or small tree with bright yellow, deciduous leaves in summer turning to red in autumn. *Cornus alba* 'Aurea' is a tough dogwood with light yellow, deciduous foliage. It responds well to a hard pruning annually in spring. The arching stems of *Weigela* 'Looymansii Aurea' carry golden-yellow, deciduous leaves margined with cerise-pink. The sight of a group of three or four spaced 1.8m (6ft) apart under a copse of mature silver birch will raise your spirits even on the wettest day of summer. *Philadelphus coronarius* 'Aureus' quickly grows to be a large shrub with deciduous leaves and creamy-white, fragrant flowers. Its foliage is bright golden-yellow until summer dulling to greenish-yellow later in the season. The finely cut, deciduous leaves of the fast-growing, red-berried elder, *Sambucus racemosa* 'Plumosa Aurea', are bronze when they first appear, turning to a bright buttery-yellow in early summer. *Physocarpus opulifolius* 'Dart's Gold' is well behaved and useful for filling a gap in a bold planting scheme. The young deciduous foliage is bright yellow but it quickly becomes, at best, green-yellow.

above Cornus alba 'Aurea', a yellow-leafed dogwood, enjoys damp conditions and will reward you with a golden glow.

Physocarpus opulifolius 'Dart's Gold' is grown mostly for its foliage, but also has pretty flowers and unusual bladder-shaped fruits later in the year.

Purple

A lot of thought needs to be given to the overall garden design when you are planning to incorporate shrubs with purple foliage. While still young, purple leaves are better described as velvet or 'royal' purple, but towards the end of summer those same leaves can look very sober in a mixed border. Deep red, bronze or purple foliage combines well with yellow leaves or flowers. Try not to include too many shades of purple because in strong sunlight they tend to compete for attention, with the smaller-leafed plants looking brighter than large-leafed plants such as *Sambucus nigra* 'Black Lace', with its bold, deep purple foliage.

In large gardens it makes sense to plant small groups of the different species out of sight from one another. You can always mix in shades of green foliage such as glossy and matt, light and dark green. High-potash fertilizers with low levels of nitrogen will enhance the colour, reducing the tendency of some shrubs to become green-purple.

The list of purple-leafed shrubs I can recommend is headed by yet another Japanese maple to add to your collection. *Acer palmatum* 'Dissectum Atropurpureum' forms a low

Sambucus 'Black Lace' is a classy elderberry. I don't usually recommend new, fashionable varieties, but this one has deservedly remained popular since it was a hit at the Chelsea Flower Show a couple of years ago, and looks as if it is here to stay.

Acer palmatum var.
'Dissectum Atropurpureum'
– one of my great
favourites for purple
foliage.

mound with deeply cut, deciduous leaves that are red-purple throughout the season. 'Crimson Pygmy' and 'Little Favourite' are some of the common names for the dwarf *Berberis thunbergii* 'Atropurpurea Nana'. Stood upright its name is almost as tall as the plant. It is deciduous with red-purple foliage and is better behaved than some of its bigger relations. Other dwarf varieties include *B. thunbergii* 'Dart's Red Lady', which has dark purple leaves during summer becoming bright red in autumn with an attractive bicoloured leaf pattern, and *B. t.* 'Bagatelle'.

The purple-leafed filbert, *Corylus maxima* 'Purpurea', is one of my favourite shrubs. I love its understated reputation. It seldom causes trouble but does suffer from greenfly. Not only are the leaves a reliable deep purple but its catkins are pale purple and the nuts are enclosed in purple-tinged husks. *Cotinus coggygria* 'Royal Purple' is a well-behaved variety of the smoke tree. In summer its wine-purple leaves appear to be translucent, gradually lightening to a bright red by early autumn.

I have to admit that by including *Weigela florida* 'Foliis Purpureis' in this category I am cheating. The deciduous foliage is best described as bronze-green, but from a distance it looks purple and I am very fond of the plant's compact habit of growth, so I have sneaked it in. Dwarf evergreen shrubs are invaluable as dot plants and *Pittosporum tenuifolium* 'Tom Thumb' is one of the best. It makes a wonderful companion for a bed of winter-flowering heathers. The young, bright green leaves turn to a deep purple during summer.

Variegated

When plants are flowering in the vicinity of variegated shrubs they should steal the attention using the variegated foliage to highlight their brilliance. It is in winter that shrubs with foliage of various colours come into their own since there is little else around to compete with their eye-catching brightness. When the foliage of a shrub is referred to as variegated further description is needed. Together with all the different greens there are leaf colour combinations in white, yellow, orange, red and purple. Even to refer to the leaf as green and yellow isn't enough. There are many shades of green and the variegation could be the result of white, cream, yellow or gold markings, which could be spots on the leaf, as with many spotted laurels, along the leaf margins, a splash in the centre or random blotches over the surface.

One of the big problems with variegated plants is their tendency to revert to the plain green foliage of the original shrub that produced the bicolour. Remove all-green branches early before they outgrow the slower variegated stems, eventually smothering the plant. Most variegated shrubs tolerate a site in partial shade. Yellow-variegated foliage tends to scorch in full sun, although holly and elaeagnus are happy in sun or shade. The spotted laurel, *Aucuba japonica* 'Crotonifolia', tolerates deep shade.

Evergreen *Euonymus fortunei* 'Emerald Gaiety' is a well-behaved shrub, pretty enough to deserve a place in any garden, easy to look after and a useful gap filler. It is particularly attractive alongside the closely related *E. fortunei* 'Emerald 'n' Gold', which has yellow rather than white margins to its leaves.

With leaves like this, who needs flowers? *Elaeagnus* x *ebbingei* 'Gilt Edge', *Pittosporum tennifolium* 'Tom Thumb' and *Cornus alba* 'Elegantissima' combine to make a stunning foliage border.

The following shrubs are definitely worth a place in your garden. *Cornus alba* 'Elegantissima' is a variegated form of the red-barked dogwood, which has summer leaf colour and striking, bright red, bare stems in winter. The grey-green leaves are margined in white. The variety *C. alba* 'Gouchaultii' has yellow-margined leaves splashed with pink. For a large, deciduous shrub with variegated foliage it is hard to improve on one of the butterfly bushes, *Buddleja davidii* 'Harlequin', whose young leaves are margined with yellow, becoming green and cream later in the season. *Elaeagnus pungens* 'Maculata' is an excellent and useful evergreen with glossy, dark green leaves well marked with rich, golden-yellow in the centre. The leaf could be described as gold with an edging of green. *Euonymus fortunei* 'Emerald Gaiety' is one of the most useful dwarf evergreen shrubs for the garden. The bright green leaves have white margins and in winter they are tinged with pink. This compact shrub can be used to form a low evergreen hedge. There are some excellent hebes but *Hebe* x *andersonii* 'Variegata' is in a class of its own. Its long, dark, evergreen leaves are streaked with grey-green in the centres and margined with creamy-white. For another good variegated hebe grow *H.* x *franciscana* 'Variegata' with its thick, short, leathery, evergreen leaves that are bright green with creamy-white margins.

Shape and texture

Even young children recognize that leaves have different shapes. My first drawings of chestnut and oak leaves are little different from those I draw now. The diversity of leaf shapes stretches the imagination. Texture ranges from gossamer to leathery, glossy to hairy and smooth to deeply veined. Often a description of the leaf is contained in the plant name as with elephant's ears (*Bergenia cordifolia*) and lambs' lugs (*Stachys byzantina*). In Latin most of the names are descriptive terms, such as *lanceolata*, which translates as lance-shaped, and *rotundifolia*, meaning rounded leaves. It is quite possible to have a fantastic and interesting garden relying solely on leaf shapes. There are enormous herbaceous plants such as phormiums with 4m (13ft) high, sword-like leaves and *Gunnera manicata* sporting 2.5m (8ft) wide leaves on 3m (10ft) high stems. Some tree-like rhododendrons have leaves 45cm (18in) long and *Ailanthus altissima* produces pinnate leaves 1m (3ft) long.

Big cities are proud of their skyline and there is no doubt they can be spectacular with domes, spires, towers, high-rise blocks and even bridges to provide a kaleidoscope of shapes and colour. In the garden you can create a dramatic horizon using leafy shrubs. Looking up a slope over the tops of plants with a curtain of sky as a backdrop can be breathtaking. The curtain is ever changing, from a dull, laden, solid grey mass to puffy, white clouds chasing each other across the canvas or a bright, startlingly blue sky. This causes the outline of the plants to seemingly harden or soften. Large, tree-like shrubs form the most dramatic outline against the sky. Cathedral-like domes of the semi-evergreen *Cotoneaster* 'Cornubia' and the large-leafed *Viburnum rhytidophyllum* will form solid clumps with a height and spread of 5–6m (16–20ft) where there is space to allow them to grow to maturity. Conifers put on a class act even in the dead of winter when dull, battleship-grey clouds are fragmented by solid shapes that appear to have been built. The many upright, spire-like branches of the fastigiate Irish yew give new meaning to the phrase 'dreaming spires'. It would be difficult to think of a skyline that cannot be emulated by a suitable shrub. Use a mixture of evergreen and deciduous plants to provide a spectacular skyline, such as a pyracantha and sambucus (elder). For a bulky evergreen with a dense mass of foliage grow camellia and elaeagnus, but to allow patches of sky to filter through, plant a large-leafed rhododendron that has a more open habit. Trees dotted through the shrubs have an important role to play, adding extra height to your skyline.

Yucca gloriosa, Eryngium giganteum and *Angelica archangelica* make an interesting collection, with the rather harsh impact of spiky flowers and dagger-like leaves softened by the yucca's mass of white flowers and the frothy greeny-yellow angelica.

The tree fern, *Dicksonia antarctica*, with its common local name of 'man fern', fooled Captain Cook. As his ship approached the shoreline at Botany Bay he saw what he thought were aborigines and feared the worst, but it was a colony of tree ferns. He wasn't attacked, but the name stuck.

Remember that tall shrubs planted on the sunny side of the garden will block out the sun during the warmest part of the day causing shade. While this is welcome on a hot summer's day, at other times it can be a problem. A good selection of leafy shrubs planted along the perimeter of a garden facing where the sun sets will stand out against the evening light.

Ideal plants for eye-catching foliage or overall shape include the following. Growing *Yucca gloriosa* is a dangerous sport as its rosette of striking-looking, tough, sword-like, blue-green leaves have lethal points waiting to deflate the posterior that backs onto them. It is ideal for a warm, sheltered site with well-drained soil. In a bed of low-growing heathers and dwarf conifers it will add interest and height. The evergreen phormiums, better known as New Zealand flax, are not shrubs but clump-forming perennials. However, they act like shrubs and I love their leaf shape so I will mention them. They require little attention but, over time, will form massive clumps that are difficult to subdue. *Phormium tenax*, with its 4m (13ft) high, broad, sword-like, dark green leaves leaves, which are blue-green on the underside, will happily mix with most shrubs of its own size. *P.* 'Maori Chief' has 1m (3ft) long leaves that tend to arch as they age. The Japanese fatsia, *Fatsia japonica*, produces marvellous evergreen leaves, which stand out in a mixed border. Young fatsia plants mix well with other shrubs but as they mature they need a lot of space and are best suited to a large border in company with hydrangeas, berberis, mahonia and buddleja.

A chestnut with attitude is *Aesculus parviflora*, known in America as the bottlebrush buckeye. Its deciduous, typically chestnut-shaped leaves are pale to mid-green. It is suitable for a mixed border where its familiar leaves will cause consternation to those garden visitors unaware of the species. Another deciduous shrub with exceptional foliage is the oak-leafed hydrangea, *Hydrangea quercifolia*. Its beauty is wasted when it is

Big, bold and autumn-flowering *Fatsia japonica* needs a sheltered spot, but in the right conditions will give unparalleled structure and charcter to the border.

planted among other hydrangeas and it will receive the attention it deserves if planted in front of evergreen shrubs with small leaves, such as ceanothus or *Choisya ternata*, the Mexican orange blossom.

Mahonia lomariifolia is one of many great mahonias. I love them all, but for foliage this species has to be the pick of the bunch. As it matures it suffers from bare legs, and a suitable 1m (3ft) high, evergreen shrub such as *Hebe* 'Mrs Winder' planted to the front will be a good companion. *Piptanthus nepalensis*, known as the evergreen laburnum, is a good strong colour all winter in warm conditions. It is semi-evergreen in my garden and will become totally deciduous in cold areas, but even so it makes a great splash of bright yellow when in flower in late spring.

A shrub boundary comprised of different plant shapes can look interesting when viewed from either side. Planting a mixed shrub bed with metre-high domed and columnar plants in front of an evergreen hedge adds depth. The hedge becomes a stage prop with the 'cut outs' appearing in the gaps between the foliage of the shrubs. By strategically placing containers of evergreen shrubs you can enhance the view, screen off unsightly buildings or frame interesting objects.

above The striking evergreen foliage of *Mahonia lomariifolia* makes it one of my favourites of this splendid family.
right *Aesculus parviflora* has large 'hands' of deciduous chestnut leaves.

Shrubs for Places

'DEUTZIA X ROSEA 'CAMPANULATA' AND CEANOTHUS 'CONCHA'

Gardens are made up of many different locations each with its own particular conditions. On the shady side of the house an area will be cast in deep shade, and where a mature tree overshadows a part of the garden there will be little or no sun. Plants tolerant of a cold, windy corner will not be the same as those that enjoy a sunny wall. There are shrubs to suit every situation, whether it's a wet or dry site or an alkaline or acid soil. Parts of the garden can be put to different uses, such as a child-friendly area or a place for entertaining, complete with patio, barbecue and comfortable seating, where fragrant, summer-flowering shrubs will be appreciated most. All these different aspects and uses will broaden the range of shrubs you can plant, giving you the chance to pick and choose from the thousands available.

Seek expert advice regarding plants to suit your requirements. It is important to know the eventual height and spread of each plant and if they have a preference for particular soil conditions. Be wary of new plants that are being promoted. They may well be hailed as superior to what has gone before but I would let someone else try them first. If they are still selling well a year later try one. The number of 'fantastic' shrubs that are never heard of after one season would fill a chapter.

Shrubs for the play area

Where there are children or visiting grandchildren the garden must be geared towards their needs. The main consideration is safety. Danger can take many forms and the following precautions should be taken.

◆ Lock up all chemicals including pesticides, fungicides, weed killers and fertilizers beyond the reach of children.

◆ Make it a policy not to plant any shrubs that are toxic in flower, leaf or berry.

◆ Avoid plants that can cause a reaction with some people, but there is a limit to how far this should be taken. Personally, I think the odd nettle sting is part of growing up and providing there is a handy dock leaf to soothe the pain it is a lesson learnt.

◆ Plant thorny shrubs such as berberis away from paths and play areas.

◆ Store all tools in a locked shed along with nails, glass bottles and bamboo canes.

◆ Make water features safe by covering the pool with galvanized mesh disguised by a layer of round river stones; incorporate moving water through a fountain on top of the stones.

◆ For your own peace of mind fence the play area with see-through mesh or chestnut pale fencing, screening it by an informal planting of shrubs, and to make escape difficult have a fastener high up on the entrance gate.

Position the main play area where it and its occupants are visible from a house window. Choose a sunny site away from cold, draughty areas, avoiding places where the wind is tunnelled such as down the side of the house. The part of the garden where children are encouraged to sow seeds and grow plants must have good, well-drained, easily cultivated soil. They, like us, will lose heart if the ground is weedy, hard and stony.

With someone else's children we refer to plant damage as vandalism. When our own children are the cause it is youthful enthusiasm. What's in a name? The damage to plants can be serious when older children play football or generally carry on. Fortunately there is a range of shrubs that can tolerate horseplay and broken branches. Top of my list of vandal-proof plants is the butterfly bush, *Buddleja davidii*. Deciduous and fast growing, it needs to be pruned every spring to keep it in good shape with maximum flowers. The long panicles of bloom appear in summer at the tips of the current growth. If a few branches get broken early in the season it is no loss, as new shoots will soon fill the gaps and produce flowers. There are lots of good varieties including *B. davidii* 'Harlequin' with variegated foliage and deep red-purple flowers.

B. x *weyeriana* produces rounded clusters of small, fragrant, yellow flowers, each with a hint of violet, during summer and autumn.

Potentillas are modest shrubs and they have a lot to be modest about. They are deciduous, managing to look dead for at least six months of the year, but when they do flower in summer the plant is usually plastered with single flowers in shades of white, yellow or red. The stems are springy and dense making the plant immune to most damage. Even if the main stem is broken it will produce new shoots the following spring. *Potentilla fruticosa* 'Dart's Golddigger' has bright yellow flowers.

For a tough, evergreen, ground-covering shrub it is hard to beat *Juniperus conferta*, the shore juniper, which apart from anything else is ideal for keeping weeds under control. It is quite prostrate and tolerant of being walked on, but there is little chance of it being sat on as its grey-green leaves are needle sharp.

Most cotoneasters can withstand abuse and *Cotoneaster conspicuus* is better than many others. It grows to 1.5m (5ft) high with small, evergreen leaves and a tangled mass of tough stems. The shiny, red fruit are non-poisonous and last until mid-winter, after

left Cotoneaster conspicuus 'Decorus' tolerates a lot of youthful enthusiasm.

below Hedera helix f. *poetarum* is strong growing and pliant.

right Vinca major responds to a light trim over with the strimmer in the spring and will survive the roughest of treatment.

which they are devoured by birds. The periwinkles, *Vinca major,* and its cousin with smaller leaves, *V. minor,* are indestructible. Low growing and evergreen, they will recover from the worst of horse play. They spread quickly by runners, forming a dense mat and flowering in summer with bright blue flowers. Ivy is useful as a ground-cover plant, withstanding constant clipping and trespassing feet. It can be a nuisance as it spreads rapidly and will climb anything it comes across. The species *Hedera helix* f. *poetarum* is different, as it normally grows as an upright, evergreen bush with orange-yellow fruit instead of the more usual black colour.

Shrubs for shady walls

The side of the house that never sees the sun is notoriously cold and possibly the most difficult site in the garden. The soil close to the base of the wall is prone to drying out in summer. With modern homes it is amazing how much builder's rubble ends up just below the soil surface close to the walls of the house. In spite of these inhospitable conditions there is no shortage of shrubs which will not only tolerate what is thrown at them but manage to thrive in it.

The lack of sun can be used to advantage. Camellia flowers suffer when morning sun follows a frost in late winter and early spring (*see pp*.132–133). When planted against a shady wall moderate frost won't harm a hardy variety such as the stunning, double, crimson-flowered *Camellia williamsii* 'Anticipation'. *Forsythia suspensa* shows off its flowers in early spring and it is as tough as old boots. It is deciduous with its bright yellow flowers fading before the leaves are produced. The young stems tend to arch, adding depth when it is planted against a wall. It looks best against a red brick wall, which sets off the yellow flowers. *F. suspensa* 'Nymans' has pale yellow flowers on young, bronze-purple shoots. *Azara microphylla* 'Variegata' is the hardiest of the azara species. It is evergreen with small, cream and dark green leaves. The clusters of greenish-yellow flowers appear on the underside of the leaves in late winter and early spring. They have a beautiful vanilla fragrance which is most appreciated when the plant is grown close to an open window. There is one hydrangea I love to grow on a shady wall and in summer it looks superb. *Hydrangea anomala* subsp. *petiolaris* clings to walls using aerial roots. It is deciduous with mid-green foliage in summer and large, white panicles made up of both male and female flowers. The leaves turn a rich, buttery-yellow in autumn leaving a tracery of bare branches on the wall.

Shrubs benefit from a moisture-retentive, but well-drained soil. Remember the roots can only travel outwards from the wall so prepare a large planting hole with a layer of well-rotted farmyard manure in the base and backfill it with a loam-based topsoil. Even though *Kerria japonica* 'Pleniflora' can't tolerate wet ground I think it deserves a bigger role in the garden. This deciduous shrub has bright golden, pompom-like flowers in spring. Prone to suckering, it will, if allowed, spread along the base of the wall.

Pyracantha (firethorn) is great value and will succeed on a cold wall. Evergreen with strong spines, it can be trained to form an espalier. The clusters of white, spring flowers are followed in autumn by yellow, orange or red berries. It dislikes being transplanted

Hydrangea anomala subsp. *petiolaris* is tolerant of shade and cold.

and is best planted as small a container-grown plant. *Pyracantha atalantioides* is vigorous with dark green leaves and bright orange-red berries, which appear in early summer. These are left untouched by birds and often last until the following spring.

One of my favourite wall shrubs is *Garrya elliptica*, known as the silk-tassel bush. It is not totally hardy and where hard frosts are common it is probably more likely to succeed on a sheltered wall that receives some sun. The variety I grow is G. *elliptica* 'James Roof' with sea-green, evergreen leaves and silver-grey, male catkins up to 20cm (8in) long in winter and early spring. G. *e.* 'Pat Ballard' produces purple-tinged catkins and G. *e.* 'Evie' has wavy-margined leaves and exceptionally long catkins.

Shrubs for sunny walls

A solid surface on the side of the house facing the heat of the afternoon sun is going to be warm, gradually cooling down in the evening as the air temperature drops. The base of the wall will be very dry, as it receives little rain and is protected by any overhang on the roof. It is an ideal aspect for a range of shrubs requiring warmth and shelter, especially those that originate in the Mediterranean area.

In fact, most shrubs benefit from the higher temperatures close to a sunny wall and this gives those of us with less than ideal climatic conditions the opportunity to grow choice plants that are not fully hardy. The flannel bush, *Fremontodendron californicum*, is, as the name suggests, from the state of California and also Arizona where hot and dry sums up the climate. In more temperate areas a sunny, sheltered wall with a well-drained soil will do very nicely. If it enjoys its home it will stay evergreen or semi-evergreen. The large, saucer-shaped, bright yellow flowers appear as early as mid-spring and will continue to flower until autumn. *F. mexicanum* has larger, deeper yellow flowers tinged red on the outside. Another shrub from California is the beautiful *Carpenteria californica* with its glossy, dark evergreen leaves. The large, fragrant, white, summer flowers have a central boss of golden stamens.

I love climbing roses providing they behave themselves. The Sam McGredy variety *Rosa* 'Dublin Bay' is not too vigorous, making it easy to grow and train. It has glossy, dark green foliage and large, bright crimson, double flowers from summer until autumn. Then there is the evergreen, climbing hydrangea from Mexico, *Hydrangea seemannii,*

right *Fremontodendron californicum* produces flowers all summer to within a few centimetres of the tip of shoots.

left Evergreen *Hydrangea seemannii* feels the cold but will thrive against a sunny wall.

whose greenish-white, fertile flowers are surrounded by a ring of pure white, sterile blooms. It is not fully hardy. *Chimonanthus praecox* is known as wintersweet, and it is hard to imagine a more descriptive common name, as it flowers in winter and has an incredible fragrance. Totally hardy, this deciduous shrub produces sulphur-yellow flowers stained with purple in the dead of winter, irrespective of weather conditions. The fragrance is freely given, making it ideal for growing outside a bedroom window.

For those with sheltered gardens in mild areas it is worth trying *Grevillea juniperina* f. *sulphurea*. The arching stems carry yellow flowers in early summer. A high-potash liquid feed in late summer and again in early autumn will help the young growths harden up before winter. For a Mediterranean look, plant *Euphorbia characias* subsp. *wulfenii* at the base of the wall. Densely packed, long, grey-green leaves give way to terminal clusters of yellow-green 'flowers'. The proper term is cyathia and these are surrounded by involucres, but if you are happy with flowers, then so am I. Whatever you call them they should be removed before they set seed or this choice shrub could become a weed in your garden. The milky sap exuded from all parts of the plant can be a skin irritant.

A shrub that deserves to be grown in more gardens is the white forsythia. *Abeliophyllum distichum* originates from Korea and it is related to forsythia, with a similar growth habit. Its fragrant, white flowers are often tinged with pink, appearing in late winter and early spring. Feed with a high-potash, liquid fertilizer in autumn to harden

Euphorbia characias subsp. *wulfenii* is a beautiful plant and aggressive with it.

Clematis armandii is everything a climber should be: easy to grow and maintain, evergreen and early flowering with a beautiful fragrance.

up the late growth before winter. A lovely climber for a warm wall is the vigorous, evergreen *Clematis armandii* with its fragrant, white flowers in early spring. At the other end of the scale is the hard-to-contain *Fallopia baldschuanica*, better known as mile-a-minute or Russian vine. Rampant in growth, this deciduous climber covers itself in pink-tinged, white flowers in summer. It can tolerate full sun when many other less aggressive, hardy climbers fade.

Shrubs for walls facing the morning sun

I have to admit to a grudging admiration for walls in this aspect. When the area is sheltered from the wind it is very pleasant to sit out in the sun with a morning coffee and the newspaper. It is even better if there is a wall to the rear of the seating area to offer shelter and privacy. Unfortunately these walls get bad press. Spring-flowering plants suffer when there is a combination of an early morning, spring frost followed by the sun. The frost freezes the flowers, which come to no harm except when the sun quickly thaws the blooms, turning them brown. Camellias are particularly susceptible. Clematis prefer to have their roots in a cool, shady spot but their heads in the sun. Plant a low-growing, evergreen shrub in front of the clematis to cast shade on the root area or mulch with a 5cm (2in) layer of gravel or composted bark.

There are plenty of excellent shrubs that will enjoy this situation. These include climbing and shrub roses such as the rich pink climbing *Rosa* 'Bantry Bay' and the wonderful *R.* 'Nevada' with pale yellow flowers ageing to pale pink. If you must have a camellia you will be most likely to succeed with *Camellia sasanqua* 'Narumigata'. It

below left Chaenomeles x superba 'Crimson and Gold' in flower at Easter.

left and above Jasminum
nudiflorum flowers in the
dead of winter, when the
garden needs all the
cheering up it can get. It can
scramble over any support,
but doesn't mind if you
prune it to keep it in check.

forms an upright, evergreen shrub with fragrant, white, single flowers with a hint of pink. As it flowers in mid- to late autumn, frost isn't a problem for the flowers, but it is slightly tender in cold, exposed gardens. Chaenomeles has many common names including japonica, quince and cydonia. One of the best varieties is *Chaenomeles* x *superba* 'Crimson and Gold'. It is deciduous, often flowering in spring before the leaves and continuing through to summer with dark red flowers and golden anthers. Another variety is C. x *superba* 'Cameo' with double, peach-pink flowers. C. *speciosa* 'Moerloosei' is vigorous with large, white flowers flushed pale pink. *Jasminum nudiflorum*, the winter-flowering jasmine, produces its bright yellow flowers on bare stems in the dead of winter. *Desfontainia spinosa* is tougher than it looks. Its crinkly, holly-like leaves are evergreen and its long, pendent, tubular, orange-red flowers are tipped with yellow and appear in summer and autumn. *Euonymus fortunei* 'Emerald Gaiety' is a compact, evergreen plant with green and cream variegated foliage. It is normally well behaved but when planted against a wall it will grow upwards for 1.5m (5ft) before realizing it isn't a climber. It is a great plant for hiding the bare legs of other climbers such as honeysuckle.

Shrubs for walls bathed in late afternoon and evening sun

Walls in this position can best be described as having a kind aspect. They make a perfect spot for relaxation with a glass of wine and good company after a day's work. There is no danger here of damage to flowers caused by late spring frost combined with early morning sun (*see pp.68–69*).

I have two walls that face the sun at the end of the afternoon and I use them to grow shrubs that are really too tender for my garden. I have occasional failures but it is surprising how many Mediterranean, South African and Australian plants have made themselves at home on these walls. From Australia comes *Acacia longifolia*, Sydney golden wattle, with dark green, lance-shaped phyllodes (instead of leaves) and bright yellow spikes of flowers in late winter and spring. The good news is that unlike most wattles it is tolerant of an alkaline soil. *Sophora davidii* is from China. Although hardy, its flowers make a better display in a sheltered situation. It is deciduous with grey-green, pinnate leaves and terminal racemes of purple, blue and white, pea-like flowers in summer. The New Zealand kowhai, *S. tetraptera*, has drooping branches with dark, evergreen leaves and tubular, golden-yellow flowers in late spring. From Asia comes the deciduous shrub *Hibiscus syriacus*. While it is hardy, long, hot summers are needed for a good show of flower. Its many varieties include 'Lady Stanley', which has beautiful, double, white flowers flushed pink and maroon in the centre, and 'Woodbridge', whose large, single, pink flowers have a deep red centre. Probably the most frequently planted variety is 'Blue Bird' ('Oiseau Bleu') with cupped, bright blue flowers with a small red centre. If, like me, your garden is in an area not blessed with long, hot summers and you have a few good frosts most winters then a wall in this position, coupled with a deep autumn mulch of bark or compost, will help hibiscus to flower.

What I can grow with ease is *Fuchsia magellanica*. *F. magellanica* var. *gracilis* is less vigorous with graceful, small, scarlet flowers with a violet 'skirt'. The cultivar 'Mrs W.P. Wood' is a favourite of mine and it is in flower outside my study window as I write. It produces masses of single flowers, each a delicate shade of pink with a white corolla (a whorl of petals in the flower).

I find it difficult to pick one rose and, while I have lots of favourites, the old glory rose, *Rosa* 'Gloire de Dijon' will always get a mention. It is vigorous with glossy, dark

above left The flowers of *Fuchsia magellanica* var. *gracilis* move like a ballerina in the slightest breeze.

above right *Hibiscus syriacus* 'Lady Stanley' sulks in a cold garden and needs to be coaxed into providing its late-summer display. These beautiful flowers make it well worth the effort, though.

green foliage. The beautifully fragrant, fully double, creamy-apricot coloured flowers are quartered showing the petals in separate swirls. Flowering is continuous from summer through to autumn. *Olearia* 'Henry Travers' used to be known as *O. semidentata* and I have raved about it for so long I am in the habit of referring to it by that name. Its evergreen leaves are long, leathery, grey-green and heavily felted white on the underside. Large, single, lilac-coloured, daisy-like flowers with purple centres appear singly in mid-summer. It is not hardy so treat it with tender, loving care.

Shrubs for the balcony

A balcony can be an alien place on which to try to grow plants. It is easy to imagine a sun-drenched, balmy, outdoor extension to your holiday apartment in sunny somewhere or other, but usually a balcony offers less than perfect condirions. Five or more storeys up, on the shady side of a tower block with the wind howling round, even on the best day, is the other type of balcony. Everything has to be grown in containers, which limits the ultimate size of the plant. Transporting pots, compost and supports up to the balcony can be a real labour of love. A container full of wet compost or soil is heavy, so check out the weight-bearing load permitted.

Shelter is crucial for most plants. Sheets of plate glass made safe by polishing or grinding the edges and bolted to the railing will offer some protection to low-growing plants. Permanent planting will have to stay outside all year unless it can be moved to overwinter elsewhere. With this in mind it is advisable to select evergreen plants that offer year-round interest, such as heaths and heathers. They like the wind in their hair as their natural habitat is windswept mountains and moors and, providing they are in a suitable compost that doesn't dry out, they will enjoy a balcony situation. *Calluna vulgaris* is properly called a heather or ling, while erica species are all heaths. Heather requires an acid soil to succeed, but some ericas such as *Erica carnea* and *E. vagans* will tolerate a slightly alkaline compost. *Calluna vulgaris* 'J. H. Hamilton' is low growing with double, bright pink racemes of flowers in late summer.

Hebe armstrongii is one of a group of low-growing 'whipcord' hebes that resembles a conifer. It is evergreen with tiny leaves and small, white, early summer flowers. *H. ochracea* 'James Stirling' has a similar habit with deep, copper-yellow foliage and small, white flowers in late spring and early summer.

If you need something tough that can withstand cold winds, dry soil and a large dose of neglect then plant *Hedera helix* 'Glacier'. The small, evergreen leaves are variegated with cream and silvery-grey. If the tips of the shoots are clipped, it will produce more side shoots 'boiling' over the side of the pot and forming a spreading, puddle-like mat over the balcony surface. It can be trained on shaped wires to form a ball, cone or hoop (*see p.112*).

Junipers are one of my favourite conifers. They are tough, reliable, not too fussy regarding soil or climate and happy to live in a cold draught. The berry is used to make gin, which is a point in its favour. *Juniperus squamata* 'Blue Star' forms a compact,

Ledum groenlandicum looks delicate but is as tough as an old boot.

right *Cornus alba* 'Elegantissima is a plant for every situation, from an exposed site to this protected corner where it is underplanted with evergreen *Vinca major* 'Variegata'. Make sure you position your pot carefully before filling it with soil, because anything this size will be too heavy to move later.

rounded bush with silvery-blue foliage. *Ledum groenlandicum*, labrador tea, is a native of Greenland so it will survive and probably thrive in most gardens. Dark, evergreen leaves and pure white, rhododendron-like flowers in late spring make this dwarf shrub a good choice as a balcony plant. Another evergreen well worth planting is the beautiful, hardy *Gaultheria shallon*, whose pink-white, urn-shaped flowers appear in late spring and early summer. It is best contained in a pot as it has a habit of wandering by means of aggressive suckers. Summer scents can be introduced with a container of herbs including sage, rosemary and lavender.

Shrubs for coastal areas

Maritime sites usually conjure up salt-laden gales and free-draining, sandy soils or else a scraping of topsoil overlying chalk. You could be forgiven for thinking that gardeners living and growing plants along the coast have problems. Well they do come across difficulties but not more than those gardening inland. There is certainly no shortage of great shrubs that will do exceedingly well in seaside gardens. With the advantage of relative freedom from frost and higher overall temperatures, many plants, considered to be tender or not fully hardy can be grown outdoors in a sheltered site.

Where there is space, plant a shelter belt of large, tough shrubs to make an interesting and colourful first line of defence, filtering and slowing the force of the wind. A suitable shrub is the deciduous *Hippophae rhamnoides*, sea buckthorn. Female plants produce masses of bright orange fruit in autumn. It will succeed in sand anywhere above high tide and once established it will layer and self seed forming a thicket.

Escallonia 'Pride of Donard' is a good, all-round, evergreen shrub ideal for seaside conditions. The bright red flowers make an impressive show throughout the summer. Other escallonias suitable for a coastal site include *E. rubra* var. *macrantha*, which has

Hippophae rhamnoides is tough enough for the most exposed site.

above With its beautiful flowers and weird but wonderful seedpods, *Colutea arborescens* is a joy for much of the year. This is another plant that looks deceptively delicate but can weather most storms.

large, dark green leaves and rosy-red summer flowers, and *E.* 'Iveyi', a big shrub with dark green foliage and large panicles of white flowers in summer and autumn. The big advantage with escallonia is being able to prune an old plant. Even when cut back to thick stumps it will rejuvenate and return to flower within a few years. *Tamarix tetrandra*, commonly called tamarisk, produces racemes of pale pink flowers in late spring on the old shoots. In late summer and autumn *T. ramosissima* 'Pink Cascade' has deep pink racemes on the current season's growth. Both of these make excellent coastal plants and, despite their ferny foliage, are hardy shrubs.

Fuchsia 'Riccartonii' is extremely hardy, making a super hedge in frost-free areas. The flowers are scarlet with dark purple 'underskirts', properly called corollas. Another great seaside shrub is the mophead hydrangea. I love *Hydrangea macrophylla* 'Deutschland' with its large heads of pink flowers. With me it has a split personality – the soil is about neutral on the pH scale and some flowers are deep pink, a few pale and the remainder are a shade of mauve. It sounds awful but is really very nice. *Colutea arborescens*, the bladder senna, is in a class of its own. Its bluish-green, pinnate leaves and racemes of coppery-yellow, summer flowers don't look hardy but it can tolerate poor, impoverished, sandy soil facing the sea. In autumn the translucent, bladder-like seed pods make a late display in the garden.

Shrubs for containers

Growing shrubs in containers is one way of making the most use of a small garden. Where there is only a hard surface with no soil, such as a balcony, back yard or patio, growing shrubs in containers is the answer. The secret of success is to choose compact plants that will be happy confined in a small space. A big advantage to growing plants in containers is that they can be moved around the garden resulting in a continuous show of colour. Heathers such as *Calluna vulgaris* can be moved out of the public gaze when the flowers die down. Move less hardy plants that require protection during winter to a more sheltered side of the house and where winters are harsh wrap the containers in bubble wrap or hessian to prevent the compost freezing and killing plant roots.

Drainage holes must be large, and covered over with pieces of clay pot or stones to hold the compost. Raising the base of the pot off the surface using bricks or purpose-made little 'feet' ensures good drainage. I prefer to use a soil-based compost such as John Innes for container-grown shrubs. It is heavier and more awkward to move than a soilless compost but less likely to dry out. The finished soil level should be 5–6cm

opposite Calluna vulgaris is a disciplined, low-growing shrub that is ideal for a container – as the season progresses you can move it around to keep it in a reasonably sunny position.

below Acer palmatum 'Chitoseyama' provides excellent autumn leaf colour and can be contained in a pot for four or five years before you let in run riot in the border.

left *Rhododendron* 'Princess Anne' forms a mound of yellow flowers in late spring and is more disciplined than many rhododendrons. It prefers some sun and shelter, so again growing it in a container is ideal as you can move it around if necessary.

(2–2½in) below the rim of the pot to make watering and feeding easier and to allow for an annual surface dressing of compost.

Evergreen shrubs, including *Skimmia japonica* 'Rubella', provide a long period of interest. This variety is a compact, male form with dark green leaves edged in red. The dark red flower buds appear in autumn and last through the winter. Another evergreen with a similar growth habit is *Hebe* 'Emerald Green' with tiny, glossy green foliage and small, white, summer flowers. For a Japanese maple suitable for a container it is hard to leave out *Acer palmatum* 'Chitoseyama', whose deciduous, bronze-green leaves colour beautifully in autumn. The Spanish gorse, *Genista hispanica*, forms a low, spiny, deciduous shrub with golden-yellow flowers in late spring and summer. As *Pieris japonica* 'Mountain Fire' does not thrive in an alkaline soil and dislikes cold winds in spring, grow it in a movable container, in a peat-based, acid compost. Its young leaves are bright red turning to a rich, chestnut-brown. Of all the dwarf rhododendrons available I have added *Rhododendron* 'Princess Anne' to the list. Its new leaves are bronze turning green and in late spring it produces funnel-shaped, pale yellow flowers.

right *Viburnum rhytidophyllum* makes a wonderful evergreen backdrop for plants in containers.

Shrubs for wet ground

There are various problems associated with a surplus of water in the ground. The site can be wet and sunny, wet and shady, wet only in winter or the dreaded waterlogged clay. The good news is that there are shrubs that will tolerate and thrive in all conditions. Perhaps the main problem area is ground, be it bog or clay, that holds water for most of the year.

Clay soil contains an abundance of nutrients but as it is composed of fine, uniformly sized particles it is without air, forming a poreless, water-retentive mass. Drains are only successful where there is a fall allowing the water to be carried away. A large soakaway made by excavating soil and filling the chamber with stone will be of short-term use collecting the water from the waterlogged site. Techniques used by forest workers include planting a tree on a raised mound of soil, so that the roots of the young tree become established before coming into contact with the waterlogged ground.

Cornus alba 'Sibirica' likes a wet soil and will put up with waterlogged conditions. In winter its bare, young stems show off the bright red bark. Pruned every year it will soon form a thicket. For a dramatic, winter display plant it in groups with the yellow-barked *C. stolonifera* 'Flaviramea'. *Aronia arbutifolia* 'Brilliant' is known in America as the red chokeberry. It is deciduous with bright red, autumn leaves, white- or pink-tinged flowers and red berries. Used as a dot plant on the edge of a bog garden it will light up the whole area in autumn. Another useful American plant for wet situations is the shallon or salal, *Gaultheria shallon*. Its glossy, dark, evergreen foliage, pink-white, spring flowers and purple fruit in autumn give it year-round appeal.

Clethra alnifolia, the sweet pepper bush, grows at my front door. Although tolerant of swamp conditions it is happier in a moist soil. In late summer and autumn the white flowers exude a wonderful, spicy fragrance. The swamp blueberry is a great treat in wet gardens. Better known as *Vaccinium corymbosum* it produces edible, sweet, blue-black berries. You may have to wear rubber boots to harvest them but it is worth it. *Viburnum opulus* is vigorous, deciduous and produces masses of fleshy, bright red fruit in autumn. *V. opulus* 'Xanthocarpum' has bright primrose-yellow fruit.

Cornus alba 'Sibirica' and *Lunaria annua* – winter Wonderland.

above Spicy *Clethra alnifolia* – the flowers are lovely, but
the scent is the real selling point.

Shrubs for dry gardens

A free-draining soil has many advantages. It is easy to cultivate, even in winter; when the soil is dry it forces plant roots to spread out in search of moisture; and light, sandy soil warms up early in the season. But in a very sunny spot a well-drained soil that lacks moisture can be the death of plants not accustomed to such conditions. The trick is to choose shrubs that grow in the Mediterranean area and love a sun-baked, dry soil.

To help a plant live happily in dry soil it is a good idea to carry out the following. Always water the shrub at ground level after planting to settle the soil around the roots and give the plant a good start. With a large, container-grown plant it may be necessary to water on a regular basis for the whole of the first season after planting. Bare-root shrubs (*see p.12*) planted in autumn or winter will need to be watered during rain-free periods. With a moist soil, mulch the area around the shrub with composted bark or gravel to reduce evaporation, but by the same token mulching on top of dry ground will prevent water penetrating through to the soil.

The following plants will do well in dry soil. *Cistus ladanifer*, the common gum cistus or rock rose, grows wild in Spain. Large, pure white flowers with yellow centres cover it in summer. *C. creticus* produces purple-pink flowers with golden stamens. I love *C.* x *corbariensis* with its deep-yellow-centred, white flowers opening from red buds in late spring and early summer. The common broom, *Cytisus scoparius*, is short lived but every spring for between six and seven years it will plaster itself with bright yellow flowers. It is a very accommodating shrub and thrives in a fairly dry, impoverished soil. *C. scoparius* 'Moonlight' is lower growing with pale, buttery-yellow flowers.

Lavender loves dry ground. Add as much sun as you like without the winter frost and you have lavender heaven. My favourite is the French lavender, *Lavandula stoechas*, with its aromatic foliage and dark purple, fragrant flowers, each with four upright bracts

Cistus ladanifer does best in the conditions it finds in its native lands, but if you can provide these it will be a constant reminder of sunny summer holidays.

like rabbit's ears. If you want very long flower stalks plant *L. stoechas* subsp. *pendunculata*, which comes from Spain and Portugal and is a slightly darker purple. *L. angustifolia* produces dense, fragrant spikes of deep purple flowers, *L. a.* 'Munstead' is blue-purple and *L. a.* 'Nana Alba' is low growing with white flowers. Cotton lavender isn't a lavender at all but it does have aromatic leaves and enjoys the same soil conditions as true lavender. Its proper name is very long, *Santolina chamaecyparissus*. In mid-summer the bright yellow, button-like flower heads are carried on long stems above the foliage. *S. chamaecyparissus* 'Lemon Queen' produces paler lemon-yellow flowers.

Romneya coulteri, the tree poppy, is a native of California and north Mexico. It will sucker like a weed if it likes the soil and the way you treat it. It is deciduous with grey-green leaves and big, white flowers with golden-yellow stamens in summer. Grown as a clump in a mixed herbaceous border it makes a startling display. I have seen *Genista aetnensis*, Mount Etna broom, in flower on the mountain it is named after. In summer the mountainside was covered with wonderfully fragrant, golden-yellow flowers, which seemed to be growing out of the rock. *Callistemon citrinus* 'Splendens' is loved by all who have seen it. Aptly called the bottlebrush, its early summer, crimson flowers are carried in spikes up to 15cm (6in) long. Phormiums, with their long, sword-like leaves are the standard architectural plant for warm, dry gardens. Commonly named New Zealand flax, they are available in a range of leaf colours but where space permits the enormous, green-leafed *Phormium tenax* is hard to beat.

Lavandula stoechas subsp. *pedunculata* making its presence felt along with *Nepeta racemosa* 'Walker's Low' and *Bellis perennis*.

Shrubs for acid soil

The scale that determines whether a soil is acid or alkaline is called the pH indicator. Acidic soil has a reading under 7 on the pH scale, and boggy, wet, badly drained ground tends to be acid. It is more difficult to lower the pH level of soil than to raise it, but in gardens where the soil is naturally alkaline a raised bed of soil with a low pH will allow you to grow acid lovers (or lime haters). The word acid has a nasty ring to it but it is a great soil for a whole range of lime-hating plants.

As there are so many excellent shrubs that thrive on acid soil I have had to curb my enthusiasm.

The rock rose, *Helianthemum* 'Wisley Primrose', flowers from late spring to mid-summer and is one of a range of superb, low, spreading varieties ideal for a rockery situation. Each primrose-yellow flower has a delightful, deep yellow centre. *Daboecia cantabrica* doesn't sound like a heather but it is commonly called St Dabeoc's heath or the cantabrian heath. It has long, glossy, dark evergreen leaves and from early summer until late autumn it produces urn-shaped, pink-purple flowers.

Acid soil and rhododendrons are like peaches and cream: they sound right together.

Pieris formosa var. *forrestii* 'Wakehurst' showing off both flower and leaf colour

Vaccinium corymbosum is another plant with a number of virtues, including edible fruit and good autumn leaf colour.

There are thousands to choose from but *Rhododendron falconeri* subsp. *eximium* has a lot going for it. It grows to be a large, bushy shrub with big leaves that are orange-brown on the underside. In late spring the pale rose-pink flowers hang in large trusses. *Enkianthus campanulatus* is deciduous with wonderful, yellow and orange autumn tints. In late spring and early summer urn-shaped, creamy-white flowers appear. To get the best results from this shrub provide it with a site sheltered from cold, biting winds. *Kalmia latifolia* 'Olympic Fire' is also called the calico bush or mountain laurel. When its crimp-shaped buds appear it becomes my favourite shrub. Wavy, evergreen foliage and pink flowers in late spring and summer make this a choice plant for the mixed border. When mature, *Pieris formosa* var. *forrestii* 'Wakehurst' makes a large, evergreen shrub with bright red new leaves gradually turning to bronze. Large panicles of urn-shaped, white flowers appear in spring. Yellowing foliage of most acid-loving plants, including pieris, is often a sign that the soil is neutral or alkaline.

If you have a soil with a pH between 5 and 6.5 then grow vaccinium. It produces the most useful berries for pies, muffins and for eating straight from the plant. *Vaccinium corymbosum* is deciduous with good autumn colouring and sweet, edible, blue-black fruit in late autumn. Another species, *V. macrocarpon*, the cranberry, is evergreen with red berries. Vacciniums are easy to grow and are at home in a shaded woodland site.

Shrubs for alkaline soil

Alkaline (or limy) soils are above 7 (neutral) on the pH indicator. There are some tricky alkaline soils, including those overlying chalk where the topsoil layer is thin. Raising the pH reading above neutral is possible by adding lime to the soil on a regular basis. 'Murphy's law' states that once you have managed to make the soil alkaline instead of acidic you will then want to grow plants that prefer an acid soil! Some gardeners get excited about acid soil and the opportunity to grow acid-loving plants such as rhododendrons. Personally I am delighted when I get the chance to garden on a limy soil because the range of plants that can be grown includes some of the finest flowering shrubs in the garden.

Ceanothus 'Concha' is a shrub I'd definitely choose for a garden with alkaline soil. Its common name of Californian lilac lets us know it likes a well-drained soil and lots of sun. It is evergreen with deep blue flowers in late spring and early summer. There are many species and varieties, including some that are deciduous, and these are mostly in shades of blue with some flowering white and, in my opinion, a few poor quality, insipid, pink varieties. Corylus avellana 'Contorta' has descriptive names like corkscrew hazel and Harry Lauder's walking stick. The young stems contort to a ridiculous degree,

My favourite weigela, W. middendorffiana deserves to be planted in every suitable garden. As long as you don't allow it to dry out it should reward you with three months' worth of beautiful flowers.

Kolkwitzia amabilis 'Pink Cloud' covers itself in flower every year in time to herald the summer.

resulting in twisted hazel branches that become evident after leaf fall. It makes a wonderful winter picture with its yellow, pendent, male catkins and the branches edged in snow or frost. *Deutzia* x *rosea* 'Campanulata' is one of those great, early summer-flowering shrubs that gives the backbone to a border. It forms a compact, deciduous plant with large panicles of pure white flowers. *D.* x *rosea* is similar in size and form with smaller, star-shaped, white flowers with a pink blush on the outside.

Beauty bush is the common name of *Kolkwitzia amabilis* 'Pink Cloud' and I wish I had been the one to think of it because it couldn't be more fitting. It is a beautiful, deciduous shrub with deep pink, bell-shaped flowers with a yellow throat in late spring and early summer. Everyone loves lilac and *Syringa pubescens* subsp. *microphylla* 'Superba' is one of the best. The good news is that the early summer, pink, fragrant flowers reappear in autumn. Another great plant for perfume is *Osmanthus delavayi*, whose terminal clusters of fragrant, white flowers in mid- to late spring make this bulky shrub invaluable. Weigelas are great shrubs for the mixed summer border. While most varieties are shades of red and pink, the flowers of *Weigela middendorffiana* are pale yellow with red throat markings and appear from late spring until mid-summer. If this species likes the conditions in your garden it will flower better than any other weigela.

Shrubs for clay soil

When gardeners get together it is always those who garden on a clay soil that get the sympathy. The main problem is its consistency. In winter it is sticky, wet and impossible to work with and come the summer it is rock hard, cracked on the surface and just as difficult to manage. The good news is that it contains plenty of nutrients. The answer to creating a more friable soil is to open up the mass of fine particles. Adding lots of clean, coarse grit, well-rotted farmyard manure and compost will, over time, improve the structure, resulting in a free-draining, moisture-retentive soil. The roots of shrubs that tolerate clay will help to open the soil. Builders can cause a lot of grief and hard work for gardeners by stripping the topsoil, selling most of it, churning up the clay subsoil and finally hiding the mess they've made under a token layer of topsoil. Where do you think the topsoil you buy to improve your clay comes from?

With a little extra attention to preparation of the soil at planting time, there are lots of shrubs that will enjoy the conditions and thrive in a clay soil. *Aralia elata* 'Aureovariegata', a late summer and early autumn flowerer, is often referred to as the Japanese angelica tree. While it is really a tree, it forms a large, deciduous, open, multi-stemmed, bushy, shrub-like plant. The stiff, spiny stems carry large, double-pinnate, long leaves. It would take more than a clay soil to slow down this quick-growing plant. Another spiny shrub is the evergreen *Berberis darwinii* whose glossy, dark green, sharply toothed leaves set off the pendent racemes of deep orange flowers in mid- to late spring. It makes a good, protective hedge. To continue the flowering programme plant the deciduous *Philadelphus* 'Sybille'. Cup-shaped, single, incredibly fragrant, white flowers are carried on arching sprays in early summer. I love all mock orange varieties but this one is small enough to fit into most gardens.

The smoke bush, *Cotinus* 'Grace', doesn't look like it would enjoy a clay soil but in such conditions it is quite happy. What it does not like is strong blasts of wind that snap its brittle branches. It is deciduous with bright green leaves that turn to a most amazing brilliant orange-red in autumn. I normally don't promote new varieties of plants, preferring to see how they turn out (*see p.xxx*), but I have been growing 'Black Lace', the new variety of *Sambucus nigra*, for two years and am happy to say I have fallen in love with it. Bred in Britain, this elderberry is as good a variety as you are likely to see for years. Deciduous, with almost black, dissected leaves and pale pink flowers in late spring, it goes on show again in autumn with clusters of deep red berries.

Elderberries love a clay soil. Here *Sambucus* 'Black Lace' plays host to *Allium hollandicum*.

There are so many roses to choose from that it comes down to personal choice. Hopefully you have the wisdom to avoid poor varieties that appear and disappear as quickly as any fragrance they might give off. One of the best modern varieties of bush rose is *Rosa* 'Irish Eyes' with good colour, disease resistance and fragrance, all made possible by the Ulster-based rose breeders the Dickson family.

Shrubs for ground cover

I have a great affection for the term ground cover. It conjures up an image of a carpet of flowering plants with the ability to suppress weeds. Using suitable plants on a prepared site, you can create such a carpet. However, it will only be possible if the ground to be planted is free of deep-rooted, perennial weeds. When preparing the ground eliminate such weeds by applying glyphosate weed killer (*see p.14*) or by covering the area for 15 months with old carpet to exclude daylight (*see p.15*). Cultivate the soil, adding bonemeal and compost or well-rotted manure.

Avoid using aggressive shrubs that after a time may become your enemy by behaving in a similar manner to the worst of weeds. For a plant that will keep light from the soil all year choose an evergreen rather than a deciduous shrub. The plants don't need to be mat forming, providing there is a canopy of leaves. A good example of weed-suppressing

Hypericum calycinum, better known as Rose of Sharon, will spread and spread, keeping weeds at bay and coping with the deep shade under trees, while providing an attractive display in itself.

Lithodora diffusa 'Heavenly Blue' will carpet the ground, preventing weed seedlings from germinating.

plants is a mature forest where the foliage is high but lack of light prevents weeds becoming established.

There are many excellent examples of good, low-growing plants that are ideal for covering the ground. *Hypericum calycinum* is better known as the rose of Sharon and it was one of the first plants I could name as a child. My neighbour's garden was full of it. Years later I met their daughter and she admitted the whole family 'kept pulling pieces off the plant and sticking them in the ground because they were so easy to root' – probably Irishman's cuttings! It is usually evergreen with dark green leaves and large, bright yellow flowers in summer and early autumn. *Lithodora diffusa* 'Grace Ward' is a prostrate, spreading, dark evergreen shrub. It covers itself with deep sea-blue flowers in late spring and early summer. *L. diffusa* 'Heavenly Blue' is better known and is similar to 'Grace Ward' but the flowers are smaller. Unlike most viburnums, *Viburnum davidii* is low growing with a height and spread of 1.5m (5ft). The three-veined, dark evergreen

Cotoneaster adpressus forms a tough mat of stems.

leaves are attractive all year. In late spring tiny, white flowers appear, followed in late summer by metallic-blue, ovoid-shaped fruit.

Cotoneaster adpressus is particularly good for covering steep banks where the mass of wiry, prostrate stems will help to hold the soil and prevent erosion. It is deciduous with small leaves that turn red in autumn. The small, red-white flowers are loved by bees and are followed by bright red fruit. If there is a lot of ground to cover and cost is a factor, then plant a periwinkle. The one I would use is *Vinca major* 'Variegata', with larger leaves than *V. minor*. It provides an endless supply of plants by rooting as it quickly spreads.

I am recommending this next plant but it is fair to say it should carry a warning notice. *Rubus tricolor* is evergreen and its creeping shoots spread at a fantastic speed. It will succeed in most soils and once it takes a hold you've got a 'friend' for life.

above and right Rubus tricolor loves to travel, covering large areas of ground once established.

Shrubs to provide shelter

It is understandable that a gardener with a new site is envious of one with a mature, established garden that is sheltered from the worst of the elements. The ideal way to break the force of the wind is to filter it through branches, twigs and leaves. Erecting a solid fence or wall causes the blast to lift over the obstacle and form turbulence on the supposedly sheltered side of the barrier. There are three types of wind that cause havoc, and these are biting, cold blasts that kill young growths, powerful blasts that smash branches and uproot plants, and, finally, salt-laden winds in coastal areas. Fortunately there are shrubs that tolerate all nature throws at them. Some of these are more functional than pretty but serve their purpose. Providing the plants with good growing conditions, such as extra care during planting, will help them to cope. It is a good idea to grow small specimens as they will acclimatize more quickly than large plants, which tend to sulk for a few seasons before deciding to start growing. Feeding in early autumn

Viburnum rhytidophyllum forms a dense evergreen shrub well capable of filtering strong blasts of wind.

Prunus spinosa can be in flower as early as late winter and produces its famous sloe berries in autumn.

with a high-potash fertilizer will firm up the young tip growth, making it more resistant to frost damage.

Where space allows, plant a few rows of hardy shrubs at a close spacing to act as a temporary first line of defence against the elements. Once the main garden plants become established these can be removed. *Cotoneaster lacteus* is a tough, evergreen shrub that makes an excellent hedge. Another useful evergreen is box, not the dwarf species used for low, dividing hedges in knot gardens but a full, tall-growing cousin. *Buxus sempervirens* 'Handsworthiensis' forms an upright, evergreen plant with stiff branches and large, dark green leaves. It makes a great hedge for filtering the wind and allowing choice plants to flourish on the sheltered side.

Prunus laurocerasus is a big name for the common laurel. If not kept under control by regular pruning it will grow to tree-like proportions with bare branches at its base. A tough plant in the prunus family is *P. spinosa*, the well-known blackthorn of hedges. Even in winter its dense mass of branches provides good protection from wind. For screening and shelter plant *Viburnum rhytidophyllum*. It makes a large, bushy, evergreen plant with arching branches. The big, dark green leaves form an outer skin all over the shrub. *V. rhytidophyllum* 'Willowwood' is similar with glossy, green, deeply veined leaves. *Photinia villosa* makes a large, bushy tree or shrub with bronze young leaves, dark green in summer before becoming orange-red in early autumn. Prune as necessary in late winter or early spring, keeping the centre of the plant open to allow sunlight in.

Shrubs for hedges

Not all hedges are planted as a means of shelter (*see p.96–97*). A living screen is ideal for hiding other gardens, unsightly views and ugly buildings. It can provide privacy and be used to break up a large garden into compartments. A boundary hedge may be needed to keep out, or in, animals, in which case impenetrable, thorny shrubs are essential. Formal hedges are those planted with shrubs that need to be clipped regularly, such as *Lonicera nitida*, beech (*Fagus*) and privet (*Ligustrum*), while informal hedges are made up of plants that only have to be clipped to keep them tidy. Many of the latter flower, including berberis, escallonia, shrub rose and fuchsia.

There are evergreen and deciduous hedges that have been popular through the ages. *Berberis* x *stenophylla* is a hedge with attitude, as it makes a bold display irrespective of weather conditions. It is evergreen with small, spiny leaves and long, arching stems

below and opposite below Rosa rugosa forms an unpenetratable barrier.

above left The spines of *Berberis* x *stenophylla* make it as fierce a plant as you could hope for in a hedge.

above right *Ligustrum ovalifolium* 'Aureum' looks best if you keep it trimmed.

covered in deep orange-yellow flowers in late spring. Prune once a year immediately after flowering. There are many good berberis and as a contrast to the previous species you could plant a hedge of *B.* x *ottawensis* 'Superba' or *B. thunbergii* f. *atropurpurea*. Both species are vigorous plants quickly making dense hedges, although the latter is more compact. Clipping should be carried out immediately after the flowers have faded. When I was a boy privet was one of the most popular hedges. For a variegated form grow *Ligustrum ovalifolium* 'Aureum', better known as golden privet, whose stems tend to be upright and vigorous. It was the first hedge I ever clipped into shape and after only ten minutes I realized it was not as easy as it looked and my efforts had only resulted in the top of the hedge having a wavy surface.

Viburnum tinus 'Eve Price' forms a compact, bushy, evergreen shrub ideal for planting as an informal screen. For the same purpose a good alternative is the similar *V. tinus* 'Pink Prelude'. *Elaeagnus* x *ebbingei* 'Gilt Edge' makes an attractive, quick-growing, evergreen hedge with green and gold variegation. It will tolerate coastal gardens where salt spray can be a problem. Hardy fuchsias are ideal for the same situation but in areas where there is little risk of frost, and *Fuchsia* 'Riccartonii' is a good choice. Its ballerina-like flowers with their scarlet tubes and dark purple 'skirts' dance their way through the summer and early autumn. *Rosa rugosa* is commonly called the hedgehog rose, ramanas rose or Japanese rose. Its fragrant, carmine-red flowers and dark red hips make it a colourful hedge during summer and autumn. For a quick-growing, easily managed, evergreen hedge it is hard to improve on *Lonicera nitida* 'Baggesen's Gold'. When regularly clipped the small, bright yellow leaves keep this plant tight and tidy.

Low-maintenance shrubs

There are many reasons for planting shrubs that need minimal pruning. Lack of time, lack of knowledge, lack of strength or lack of a head for heights are all bona fide short comings. There is no shortage of suitable plants, but care must be taken that you are not the cause of an eventual need to cut. Plant density is critical. Insufficient research and information on the ultimate height and spread of the shrub may result in close planting, leading to overcrowding and the need to thin. Positioning the plant close to a vertical obstacle such as a wall or where the branches eventually overhang a path or adjoining property will necessitate surgery, or perhaps butchery is a better description. Even during the lifetime of the best-behaved shrub it will need the occasional crossing branch removed to prevent rubbing. Diseased stems, suckers from below a graft or reverted branches on variegated plants are all reasons for the occasional use of secateurs.

Magnolia stellata 'Royal Star', the star magnolia, is one of the best known of this genus. Its compact habit makes it suitable for most gardens and it will succeed in an

Magnolia stellata 'Royal Star' will need a 'short back and sides', but nothing more demanding than that.

alkaline soil. When it comes to pruning magnolias there is a lot of nonsense written and talked on the subject. It is not that you should not prune them but there should be no need. 'Royal Star' is deciduous with mid-green leaves and pale pink flower buds, which open before the leaves in mid- to late spring. Its pure white, star-shaped flowers are made up of more than 15, thin, strap-like petals.

Rhododendron luteum is a deciduous azalea with hairy, mid-green leaves. The sticky, soft yellow, fragrant, funnel-shaped flowers appear in late spring and early summer in trusses of at least six flowers. Correctly spaced in a suitable situation you will be able to enjoy it for a lifetime without any pruning. There are more spectacular camellias than *Camellia* x *williamsii* 'Saint Ewe' but I love its simplicity. Its glossy, evergreen leaves are a perfect backdrop for the single, rose-pink flowers in spring. In my garden I have had a plant growing beside a window for 25 years and in all that time it only sees the secateurs when the flowers are cut for indoor decoration.

Camellia x *williamsii* 'Saint Ewe' is simply effective and has the decency to drop its flowers once they are past their best, rather than hanging on to unattractive brown petals as some camellias do.

Witch hazels are magic in flower. In the dead of winter they burst into bloom with incredible fragrance. *Hamamelis* x *intermedia* 'Moonlight' is deciduous with its bright green leaves turning buttery-yellow in autumn. The pale yellow flowers resemble lemon zest, appearing in mid- and late winter, irrespective of weather conditions. Give it plenty of space to grow and avoid having to move it when it is large. All witch hazels dislike being transplanted. *Callistemon citrinus* 'Splendens' is the well-known Australian bottlebrush. I would have to ask why would anyone want to prune such a magnificent plant? Its arching stems produce pink-red young shoots and in early summer masses of crimson 'bottlebrushes'. A cylinder of hard seed capsules remains for years along the older stems.

Anyone who has enjoyed growing a tree peony will know what I mean when I refer to it as a classy shrub. *Paeonia lutea* var. *ludlowii* is very happy left unpruned. It is deciduous with bright green foliage. The cup-shaped, bright yellow flowers are up to 12cm (5in) across, appearing in late spring. Avoid biting, cold, drying winds. *Fothergilla gardenii*, the witch alder, is another shrub that should never be shown cutters. It is a low-growing, deciduous plant with dramatic autumn leaf colour.

above and right Paeonia lutea var. *ludlowii* forms a choice flowering shrub.

Shrubs for fragrance

Scent, perfume, fragrance and aroma are words used to describe plants with a pleasant smell. We immediately think of the flower as the source but leaves can also make your nose take notice. There are equally descriptive terms for a less appealing smell such as pungent, stinking and putrid, as in 'stinking hellebore' and 'stinking iris'. But, it is a personal thing and not everyone has the same preferences. I love the spicy fragrance exuded by the flowers of *Clethra alnifolia*, the sweet pepper bush. Wilma (my wife and head gardener) isn't so keen, preferring the perfume of an old-fashioned rose or sweet pea blossom. The scented foliage of *Choisya ternata* is enjoyed by many gardeners but avoided by the rest.

There are plants such as sarcococca that are generous with their fragrance, which is expelled from their flowers and carried on the air. Others are more secretive, holding it for the unsuspecting 'sniffer' who suddenly gets a double-barrelled shot of heady scent.

Lavandula stoechas is a wonderfully aromatic lavender.

Sarcococca confusa will welcome you into the garden on the bleakest winter's day.

Brushing against shrubs with aromatic foliage is another way to smell their scent and if you walk along a narrow path edged with lavender your clothes will carry the aroma for days. Plants produce perfume to attract pollinating insects but there is no reason why you can't enjoy it at the same time.

Lavandula angustifolia 'Hidcote' is traditionally known as English lavender, and its grey-green foliage is highly aromatic. The dark violet, fragrant flowers are held above the leaves on long stalks during mid- to late summer. The leaves of French lavender, the exquisite *L. stoechas*, are just as aromatic. The grey-green, fragrant foliage is evergreen. It flowers from late spring to late summer with dark purple flowers topped with four, long, vivid purple bracts giving, the flowers their characteristic look.

I couldn't possibly talk about scent in the garden without mentioning a rose that virtually started the perfume industry. In Turkey, the double, pink flowers of *Rosa* x *damascena* 'Trigintipetala' are harvested in the early morning before sunrise and transported to a distillery where the essential oil is extracted to make Attar of Roses. This variety may be difficult to obtain, but the next best thing is *R.* x *damascena* 'Quatre Saisons', which is easily available. Its highly fragrant flowers appear in early summer and, as a bonus, again in autumn. A great shrub for a sunny wall is the deciduous pineapple broom, *Cytisus battandieri*, which has the unmistakable scent of pineapple. Its deep yellow flowers appear from mid- to late summer. It does best in a sheltered position. My favourite winter-flowering shrub is *Sarcococca confusa*, the Christmas box. The fragrance of its clusters of small, white flowers will bowl you over when you are 6m (20ft) from the plant. If you have the space, go for a group of three.

Shrubs for berries

Fruit and berries are an essential part of the garden scene. They provide colour, shape and interest throughout the year, especially in autumn, winter and spring. During winter they are the staple diet for lots of wildlife, bringing a parade of birds to the garden. Pollination is necessary for the production of seed and berries and with some plants male and female clones are needed to guarantee the berries. Other shrubs, such as *Skimmia japonica* subsp. *reevesiana* 'Robert Fortune', are hermaphrodite, with male and female flowers on the same plant.

A word of caution: many berries are toxic. Their bright colours are an obvious attraction for children and the fact that they are eaten by birds is no guarantee of safety. The red arils (berries) of yew are enjoyed by birds and although the flesh is edible the seed is poisonous. The seed passes through the bird undigested. Where there are children, make certain all berrying plants are edible.

Perhaps the most spectacular of all rosehips – *Rosa moyesii* 'Geranium'. I love their warm glow on a sunny autumn evening.

Callicarpa bodinieri var. *giraldii* 'Profusion'; even Ford couldn't match this for metallic pink.

The tiny, white, spring flowers of *Gaultheria mucronata* give way to clusters of shiny fruit. A selection of varieties will result in white, pink, lilac, red and magenta berries. The guelder rose, *Viburnum opulus*, has clusters of white flowers that are replaced by bright red, fleshy berries in autumn. The variety *V. opulus* 'Xanthocarpum' is similar with startlingly bright yellow fruit. Eating the fruit of any viburnum can cause a stomach upset. *Elaeagnus umbellata* makes a big shrub whose young leaves are silvery-green maturing to glossy mid-green. Its flowers appear in late spring and early summer and in autumn comes the shiny red fruit.

Question: when is a tree not a tree? Answer: when it is the dwarf *Sorbus reducta*. When the late spring flowers are over crimson berries appear, turning to white flushed rose-pink. If you want fruit that will be a talking point in your garden or in an indoor arrangement then grow *Callicarpa bodinieri* var. *giraldii* 'Profusion'. Its common name is beauty berry and it certainly lives up to it, as in autumn it produces masses of bead-like, metallic, shiny, deep violet fruit. I marvel at all rose hips especially the big tomato-shaped fruit of *Rosa rugosa*. Even more spectacular is the beautiful shrub rose *R. moyesii* 'Geranium'. The rose hips are large, orange-red and flagon-shaped, hanging like jewels on the bare stems from autumn until early winter.

Shrubs for autumn foliage

I love all the seasons, but I always prefer the one I am in at the time. Autumn is a time to remember all the bright, perhaps gaudy colours of summer, when the more muted but memorable shades of leaf colour are all around. As the firework display draws to a close the garden palette will turn to the paler shades of winter with skies darkening early and your breath preceding you as you work outside. The intensity of leaf colour can change from year to year with some shrubs. After a wet summer or a cold period in early autumn some may perform poorly but others are totally reliable with a cast-iron guarantee of superb colour that only varies in commencement date, not in beauty. Yellow, orange, cerise, red, scarlet or purple foliage are commonplace from late summer until leaf fall.

The foliage of *Cotinus* 'Flame', the smoke bush, turns from light green to an

Rhus typhina 'Dissecta' is not the best behaved plant in the world, but this autumn display makes me overlook its misdemeanours.

Fothergilla major is another 'good value' shrub – easy to take care of and providing pretty white flowers, a delicate scent and superb autumn colour.

incredible red with a hint of orange in early autumn. The display can last until the first frost. Books have been written on Japanese maples with more than a few chapters devoted to autumn leaf colour. Many become red-purple in late summer but *Acer palmatum* 'Dissectum', with its finely cut leaves, turns to a rich gold in early autumn. The deciduous green leaves of *Fothergilla major* take on glorious shades of yellow, orange and red. For the richest colours grow it in full sun. *Euonymus europaeus* is better known as the spindle bush of British hedgerows. *E. europaeus* 'Red Cascade' is deciduous with dull green leaves that are transformed to bright red. *Disanthus cercidifolius* is a rounded, dense, shrub with bright rosy-red flowers in mid-autumn. As the flowers finish, the leaves turn to orange, red and purple, lasting until the first gale or frost. The stag's horn sumach, *Rhus typhina* 'Dissecta', can be a nuisance as it is prone to suckering badly, but all is forgiven in autumn when its pinnate leaves take on brilliant shades of orange and bright red.

Shrubs for under trees

The difficulty of growing plants under trees is a constant moan wherever gardeners gather. In truth there are plenty of shrubs that will grow quite happily in this situation, though certainly there are problems. Soil can be permanently dry, there may be deep shade, large drops of rain from leaves may damage small plants and tree roots close to the soil surface will make it difficult to dig a planting hole. Deep, annual surface applications of leaf mould or compost will improve the soil conditions and help to retain moisture. If the head of the tree can be raised by removing some of the lower branches, more daylight will get to the plants below. Evergreens constantly cast shadow, whereas deciduous trees allow light and sun to filter through for part of the year.

The low-growing, creeping habit of *Gaultheria procumbens*, wintergreen, makes it ideal for growing under trees, and as an added bonus its evergreen leaves smell of wintergreen when they are crushed. White or pale pink flowers appear in summer. *Ruscus hypoglossum*, is clump forming with glossy, evergreen leaves, which are not leaves at all. Red berries appear in late summer lasting through most of the winter. It will tolerate deep shade but looks a bit dull where there is little natural light. Heathers prefer an open, sunny position, but *Erica carnea* will tolerate light shade, even under large deciduous shrubs. Providing the soil is free-draining, euphorbias also cope with light shade and the competition from tree roots.

Daphne laureola, commonly called the spurge laurel, is an excellent evergreen shrub for deep shade in winter when it produces fragrant, green-yellow flowers until early spring, followed by black fruit. The glossy, dark green, leathery leaves look good all year.

left Erica carnea – this variety is 'Pirbright Rose' – provides pretty ground cover and copes well with the shady conditions.

Euphorbias planted under trees look good and tolerate the competition for root space.

D. laureola subsp. *philippi* is compact with deeper yellow flowers. *Skimmia japonica* subsp. *reevesiana* has narrow, tapered, pale evergreen foliage. The large clusters of red berries last well into the winter and, even though a single species will produce berries, I love to see a group of three or more. For a big, bold, evergreen shrub, plant *Aucuba japonica*, the spotted laurel. It can tolerate deep shade. Female plants produce bright red berries in autumn. A. j. 'Crotonifolia' is female with attractive leaves freckled with bright yellow.

Shrubs for topiary

Love it or hate it, a well-shaped piece of living sculpture is fascinating to look at. Personally I am delighted to see good examples in other gardens, but doubt if I would have the patience to shape a plant. I can hardly wait until the hairdresser has cut my hair.

Not every plant can tolerate the constant clipping needed to form a shape. Generally speaking, shrubs with small leaves perform better than those with large foliage. Ideally they should be evergreen with the leaves closely spaced. Steady growth over a long period is required and is best achieved by regular feeding with a balanced fertilizer and watering. In this day and age when everything a gardener could possibly want is available, there are wire frames pre-shaped for the topiary of your choice. All you have to do is place the frame over the plant and cut off any growth that escapes it.

Photinia x *frazeri* 'Red Robin' has fairly large evergreen leaves that, when young, are a fiery-red fading to bronze in late summer or autumn. It looks quite dramatic when it is clipped to form a 1.8m (6ft), bare-stemmed standard with the head shaped into a sphere. It is difficult to keep it compact without sacrificing the red foliage early in the summer. Best of all for topiary is the well-known box, which has been used as dwarf hedging for centuries. *Buxus sempervirens* 'Suffruticosa' is compact, evergreen and slow growing.

right Photinia x *fraseri* 'Red Robin' clips well into a standard topiary pompom, with box hedging beneath.

below Box such as this *Buxus sempervirens* 'Suffruticosa' is the traditional plant used to mark out the beds of knot gardens.